# Spanish Verbs Genius.

## Everything you need to conquer Spanish verbs and speak Spanish correctly.

★Every Different Spanish Verb Type,
Detailed and Explained.

★ The Lock-Step Learning Method
for Mastering All Spanish Verbs & Tenses

★ The 151 Essential Spanish Verbs to Study
each with translation and conjugation guide

★ Fast Track your learning of Spanish verbs
with this clever guide as your companion.

By: Peter Oakfield

Riverbridge Books

ISBN 978-1-9160398-1-0

This edition published in the United Kingdom by
Riverbridge Books
192 Leckhampton Road, Cheltenham GL53 0AE   U.K.
Copyright © Peter Oakfield

About the author:
Peter Oakfield lives in the west of England and also writes about memory and topics related to the Spanish language, as well as dual language Spanish short stories. His other books include:

*How to learn - Spanish - French - German - Arabic - any foreign language successfully.*
 *and*
*How To Transform Your Memory & Brain Power: Power-Learn, Memorize & Remember Anything.*
*and*
*How I Learned To Speak Spanish Fluently In Three Months: Discover How You Can Conquer Spanish Easily The Same Way.*
*and*
*Dual Language First Spanish Reader. Spanish-English Short Stories for Beginners*
*and*
*Dual Language Spanish Reader. Parallel Spanish-English Short Stories. Level Beginner to Intermediate*
*and*
*Spanish Verb Perfect: Fully Conjugated Models for Every Type Of Spanish Verb*

**Table of Contents**

# Introduction

**Spanish verbs.**
The rewards to be gained from learning Spanish are enormous, not just from the pleasure of being able to speak it but also from enjoying the literature and the culture.

But in order to be able to speak Spanish well it is essential to have a good knowledge of the verbs and to master their use. The verbs are the keystone of each and every sentence. They are the words that make things happen and without them a sentence would be just a collection of words without vitality and direction.

Accordingly for those learning Spanish, it is just as important to understand the verbs and to learn to use them, as it is to learn vocabulary generally. However, bearing in mind that there are 6 different persons for the conjugation of each tense, that there are 8 different tenses (i.e. including the imperative and the subjunctive, the latter having two forms, so 9 conjugations) as well as the compound tenses, it may at first seem that there is much to be mastered.

Luckily though, the work is in reality much less than might be imagined if it is approached in the right way and if you have the right tools and information. For example, as you will discover in this book the compound tenses are very easy to learn; there is much regularity in the forms of the verbs; and whilst there are certainly seeming irregularities with many types of verbs, most of the irregular verbs in fact follow a rule or at least a sort of pattern; and the number of truly irregular verbs without any obvious pattern is really very small. And even these can be mastered swiftly if the clever learning techniques, which will be explained in this book, are applied.

Accordingly the scheme of this book is to present the subject as a workbook to fast track you to success and fluency with the Spanish verb. There are in four important parts in this book as follows.

# Part 1 Understanding the Spanish Verb
You will discover here all the Spanish verb forms that you need to know so as to be able to understand and to learn them, however and whenever they may be encountered or required. It will be appropriate

for student at every level from beginner to advanced, and can be used both for learning and for simple reference purposes.

You will find full explanations of every type of regular verb; and of every type of irregular verb; both those that may follow a pattern in their irregularity, and also of all the other completely irregular verb forms.

## Part 2 Mastering and Recalling Spanish Verbs and Tenses

**Essential Memorizing Techniques for Memorising Spanish Verbs; the Lock-Step Learning Method for Mastering Spanish Verbs & Tenses; and also Memorising tips for different Spanish verb conjugations.**

It is not enough to be able to understand Spanish verbs when they are encountered. It is essential also to be able to recall and to be able to conjugate them whenever required. Accordingly special attention has been given to the importance of learning and memorising Spanish verbs, and there are 3 Chapters in this part of the book devoted specifically to proven memory techniques for learning and recalling verbs and their conjugations, including the Lock-Step Method for Spanish Verbs and Tenses, that will be found to be particularly valuable. The last of these chapters details numerous memorising tips patterns and pointers for different types of Spanish verb tenses.

## Part 3 The Most Useful and Essential Spanish Verbs:

**The 151 most useful Spanish verbs.**

By way of a further aid to the mastery of the Spanish verb, this book contains a collection of **the 151 most important and essential Spanish Verbs** for the student to learn. When you know these verbs you will be able to to speak Spanish more than comfortably in all everyday situations. Every one of the 151 is provided with a translation and a conjugation guide.

Learn the 151 and you will be able to make yourself understood and to get by reasonably in the Spanish language in all everyday situations.

**How To Use This Book**

You can use this book either for regular learning, or as a reference when uncertain as to a verb or its conjugation. However when learning the verbs initially (and for that matter, when learning the Spanish language generally) keep in mind the value of regular daily study. The importance of this cannot be overstated. Regular work at the study of the verbs (and especially the practical use of them) at least once a day will yield much better results than occasional study, for example just once a week, even if the amount of time devoted to the work is the same (e.g. by having one really long session at the weekends).

With the aid of this book you will soon be able to command the Spanish verb and achieve your goal of fluency with the Spanish language. Good luck with your study.

If you have any comments you are welcome to email me at p.oakfield.spanish@gmail.com

*Part One: Understanding the Spanish Verb*

## Chapter 1.
## How To Pronounce Spanish Verbs Correctly

Knowing how to pronounce Spanish verbs, which requires a knowledge of how to pronounce Spanish letters and words, will help you to learn and remember the conjugations of the verbs more easily as will be seen. It will also help you both to speak the language correctly so that you will be understood, and in turn to be able to understand what is said to you.

The following simple rules are therefore an essential preliminary before Spanish verbs are studied.

### 1. How to pronounce the consonants.

**b** Sounds much as it does in English, but slightly softer.

**c** Sounds like the **c** in Call, except where it appears before the letters **e** or **i**. In these cases the **c** is pronounced **th** as in Think.

**d** Sounds much as it does in Dog, but is slightly softer. However where the **d** is at the end of a word or between two vowels the sound of the **d** is nearer to TH as in Think.

**f** Sounds as it does in English

**g** Sounds like the **g** in Goat, Got or Get, except where it appears before the letters **e** or **i**. In these cases the **g** sounds like the ch in Loch

**gu** Where **gu** appears before either **e** or **i** it sounds like **g** in Goat or Get and the **u** is then silent. However when the u after g has two little dots, ü, (a dieresis) then the u is pronounced. It sounds like Gooay as in bilingüe-(bilingual)

**h** This letter is always silent.

**j** Sounds like the **ch** in Loch (ie the same as the G before the letters e o i).

**k** Sounds like **k** in English. E.G. As in Kick.

**l** Sounds like the **l** in English E.G. As in Lot.

**ll** Sounds like the **lli** in Million.

**m** Sounds as it does in English. E.G. As in Metal.

**n** Sounds as it does in English. E.G. As in Now.

**ñ** Sounds like the **ny** in Canyon

**p** Sounds as it does in English. E.G. As in Pit.

**q** This letter is **always** followed by the letter U and QU is pronounced like the K in Keen

**r** Where the **r** appears at the end of a word or between vowels it is pronounced like the R in Rig. At the beginning of a word the letter R is somewhat rolled.

**rr** The double **rr** is rolled almost with a purring sound.

**s** Sounds like the **s** in Snake. Think of a hissing snake. Note that the s should not be pronounced like the s in Treasure.

**t** Sounds like the **t** in Test. It is pronounced crisply.

**v** Has a sound somewhere between v and b and often just a less vigorous b sound.

**y** Sounds like the **y** in Yank. The y is only a consonant when it appears at the beginning of a word or syllable.

**z** Sounds the **th** in Think.

### 2. How to pronounce the vowels.

**a** Sounds like the **a** in Apple.

**e** Sounds like **ay** in Hay.

**i** Sounds like the **ee** in Need.

**o** Sounds like the **o** in Cope.

**u** Sounds like the **oo** in Loop.

**y** Is only a vowel when it is on its own ( Y = and) sounds like the **ee** in Need, or at the end of a word.

### Learn the sounds by listening and repeating.

To begin to grasp and to learn to speak the sounds correctly it is important not just to read about them (and bear in mind that written guidelines can only be an approximation) it is essential to listen to them as well. The best way is to listen repeatedly to audio recordings with a transcript, paying attention to each and every word, and repeating each sentence or phrase after you have heard it.

### 3. How to place the stress in the correct place with Spanish words.

Knowing how to place the stress correctly when speaking a Spanish word is of great importance, but luckily the rules are quite simple.

First: If the word has a letter with a written accent over it ( EG **á** or **é** or **í** or **ó** or **ú**) the stress or accent is applied to the letter so written. Examples: m**é**dico, p**á**rroco, combinaci**ó**n, est**é**ril.

Second: If the word has no written accent but ends in a consonant (but not if the word ends in **n** or **s**) then the last syllable is stressed. Examples: comerci**a**l, desped**i**r, sal**u**d, prens**i**l.

Third: If the word has no written accent but ends with a vowel, or with **n** or **s,** then the syllable before the final syllable is stressed. Examples: tort**i**lla, br**a**zo, c**a**mbio entr**a**da.

How essential is it to know where the stress should be? Would it for example matter if the word were not correctly pronounced? It is in fact very important to have the stress in the right place. Consider the following two Spanish words ( the stress is shown bold):

Esp**e**ro = I hope/wait
Esper**ó** = He hoped/waited

As will be seen the different stress for each word results in a different meaning despite the similarities. The position of the stress can also explain a change in the spelling and pronunciation in the stem of a verb.

# Chapter 2.
## Understanding the language of verbs

Like many subjects, verbs have some specialist words which are used to refer to different aspects of verbs or the way in which they are used. These words are a form of shorthand which makes it easier to describe what is being spoken about, instead of having to use a longer explanation each time. Set out following are the most important examples of such words, with a short explanation of each.

There is no need to try and memorise these terms. Just read them over from time to time. Also whenever you come across any of the words in this book, you can check back quickly to refresh your understanding as to their meaning.

Note that the brief notes for each of the verbs are intended only as an introduction. All the different verb types will be dealt with fully further on.

**Verb**: This is included only for the sake of completeness. A verb is a word which indicates the action in a sentence. E.G. The dog **barked**. He **read** the book.

**Infinitive verb**: The infinitive of the verb is the verb in its basic form, before it has been altered in any way. All possibilities are still open as to the what will be done with it. In English the infinitive is recognizable because it includes the word "to". E.G. **To bark, to read**. In Spanish the verbs in the infinitive do not include the word "to" separately. The idea of the "to" is implied. All Spanish verbs in the infinitive end with the letters **ar**, or **er**, or **ir**.

**Active**: This indicates that the subject of the verb carries out the action referred to by the verb. E.G. The boy ran.

**Passive**: This indicates that the subject of the verb suffers the action referred to. E.G. The boy was stopped.

**Reflexive verb**. This is a verb in which the action turns back in some way on the subject. E.G. He stopped himself. English does not use reflexive forms much but in Spanish they are quite common. In Spanish a reflexive verb in the infinitive is recognizable by having the letters **"se"** at the end. Examples: despedirse (to take one's leave: to say goodbye). Peinarse (to comb one's hair).

**Persons**: the different persons who may be the subject of the verb:
First person singular: I. In Spanish Yo
Second person singular: You (ie only one person). In Spanish Tú
Third Person singular: He. In Spanish Él or Ella if female. Usted (formal way of saying "you" to one person)
First person plural: We. In Spanish Nosotros or Nosotras if all are female.
Second person plural: You (ie more than one person). In Spanish Vosotros or Vosotras if all are female,
Third person plural: They. In Spanish Ellos or Ellas if all are female. Ustedes (formal way of saying "you" to more than one person)

**Conjugate**: to conjugate means to give the various inflections or parts of the verb in a desired tense. For example, taking the English verb 'to give', and conjugating it in the present indicative tense.
First person singular: I give
Seond person singular: You give
Third person singular: He gives
First person plural: We give
Second person plural; You give
Third person plural; They give

**Present-Particle ('Present-P')**: In English where the form of the verb ends with the letters ING, it is called the Present-Participle when it is part of a verb. E.G. The dog was barking: 'barking' is here the Present-Participle.

The Present-Participle may also be used as a noun in English. For example: Running is a healthy sport. Smoking is bad for you. Etc. A Present-Participle used in this way it is known as a gerund – a verbal noun. This does not occur in Spanish where the Present-Participle would not be used as a noun. (In Spanish the infinitive would be used instead: E.G. Smoking is bad for you.= El fumar es malo para ti.)

In Spanish the Present-Participle of a verb will generally end as follows:

Verbs ending in AR: drop AR and add..."ando". E.G. Hablar...Hablando = Speaking

Verbs ending in ER: drop ER and add...."iendo". E.G. Correr...Corriendo = Running

Verbs ending in IR ..drop IR and add..."iendo". E.G. Partiendo = Leaving/departing

Note that there are some irregular Present-Participles.

**Past-Participle ('Past-P')** : The verb is described as the Past-Participle when it is in the form in which it is added to another verb to give an indication of the past. E.G. He has stopped.

In Spanish the Past-Participle of the verb will usually end as follows:

Verbs ending in AR: drop AR and add "ado". E.G. Hablar ..Hablado = Spoken

Verbs ending in ER drop ER and add "ido" E.G. Correr...Corrido = Run

Verbs ending in IR drop IR and add "ido". E.G. Partir...Partido = Left/departed

Note that there are some irregular Past-Participles

Note that the Past-Participle may sometimes be used with the verb 'to be', not as part of the verb expressing the action, but as an adjective; and in these circumstances it will, like any adjective in Spanish, have to agree in gender and number with the noun which it modifies.

**Personal pronouns** for verbs in English and Spanish. (See Persons above)

I = Yo

You = (singular intimate form) Tú

He = Él. She+Ella.

You (singular: formal address) = Usted

We = Nosotros or if all are female Nosotras

You (plural intimate form) = Vosotros or if all are female Vosotras

They = Ellos or if all are female Ellas

You (plural: formal address) = Ustedes

**Verb Stem:** the form of the verb with the ending (AR, ER or IR) removed. For example: the infinitive of the Spanish verb Tomar (to

14

take) with the infinitive ending AR removed, is Tom. This is called the stem, and different forms of the verb are created by adding letters onto the stem. For example: Tomaba (I/he was taking).

**Verb ending:** the infinitive endings for all Spanish verbs are (as indicated above): **ar**. or **er**, or **ir**. The infinitive of every Spanish verb will end in one of those ways. For the various tenses the endings will be different as will be seen.

**Tense:** This word refers to the verb in a form which indicates the time of the action. E.G. The present, the past, the future etc.

**Present Indicative tense:** The verb is making a simple statement as to what is actually happening at the moment. E.G. He drinks. She reads. The dog barks.

**Past historic or preterite tense:** The verb is expressing a completed action. E.G. He read the book. They paid the bill. She scored the goal.

**Imperfect tense:** The verb is expressing something which was going on at some time in the past, but not completed, or which occured regularly. He was reading the book. They were paying the bill. She was scoring the goal. He was working every day last week.

**Future tense:** The verb is expressing something, which will certainly happen in the future. E.G. He will read the book. They will pay the bill. She will score the goal.

**The conditional:** The verb is expressing the idea of something in the future, which is uncertain. It suggests that the something might happen if some condition were to be met. E.G. He would read the book (if you asked him to do so). They would pay the bill (if they had the money). She would score a goal ( if she is allowed to play).

**Mood:** The form of the verb that expresses the mode or manner or state of the action. E.G. **Indicative mood:** the verb when it just affirms or denies something. E.G. The boy ran. Other moods: The imperative and the subjunctive: see below.

**Imperative mood:** The verb when it expresses a command or advice. E.G. Shut up. Begin at once. Stop that.

**Subjunctive mood**; The verb when it expresses condition, hypothesis or contingency. E.G. If I were you. He may have arrived. He should have arrived. In English the subjunctive mood is not much used but in Spanish it is in common usage.

**Compound tense:** A verb used together with another to form a single tense. In Spanish the verb Haber is mostly used only as an auxillary verb to form compound tenses. E.G. I have read. They should have paid the bill. She had scored the goal. However there are certain expressions related to the verb Haber which will be seen ahead. E.G. Hay: there is, there are, etc.

**Irregular verbs:** Verbs which do not conform to the general rules for the conjugation of verbs with their particular ending.

**Radical Stem changing verbs:** These are verbs which have a change in the vowel of the stem when the stress falls upon the usual vowel in the verb stem.

**Othographic and Euphonic changes in verbs:** These are verbs which may not be fully irregular but which have a change to accommodate the sound of the tense being used. With minor exceptions the sound follows what would be expected with the usual rule for the verb, or produces a more comfortable sound.

# Chapter 3.
## Conjugating Spanish Verbs: the different persons.

The different persons who may be speaking have already been introduced above. Yo, Tú, Él (Ella), Usted (Ud.), Nosotros (Nosotras), Vosotros (Vosotras), Ellos (Ellas), and Ustedes (Uds.).

Some comment with regard to the use of Usted and Ustedes is necessary so as to make the use of the appropriate verb ending clear.

The word Usted is a contraction the words Vuestra Merced, meaning Your Grace. In the past in Spanish this form of address became common and because it is an address in the third person, it follows that the verb ending for it is also that for the third person. In other words it is exactly the same as for Él where there is one person (Usted); or the same as Ellos where there is more than one person (Ustedes).

This is much the same as it would be in English when addressing, for example a Judge. E.G. Not "you know" but "Your Honour knows"; or Royalty: E.g. "Your Majesty is welcome" and not "you are welcome".

The use of Usted was widespread at one time for addressing almost anyone other than children and family relations. It was used as a mark of respect, and even now it is not uncommon, but the use is diminishing, and the use of the familiar or more intimate Tú and Vosotros, is much more likely. The student should know how to use the correct verb ending for either style of address, and when in doubt it will be best to use Usted, as formal politeness is never going to cause offence. However when addressed as Tú or Vosotros, it will be appropriate to reply with similar address.

The conjugations of verbs in this book will always be set out in the following order, namely :
1st person singular (Yo),
2nd person singular (Tú),
3rd person singular (Él (Ella), Usted (Ud.)),

1st person plural (Nosotros (Nosotras)),
2nd person plural Vosotros (Vosotras),
3rd person plural (Ellos (Ellas), Ustedes (Uds.)).

For this reason the personal pronouns will not always appear next to the verb conjugations where they are set out in this book. Where they do not appear there is no need for them, because they will always be the same and the conjugations will always be in the same order.

# Chapter 4.
# The Present Tense

The present tense is a simple statement of what is occurring at the moment: the verb is referring to some action that is going on as the person speaks, or is something that is generally occurring.

E.G. He reads: Él lee. She speaks: Ella habla. They eat: Ellos comen. He walks to work: Él camina al trabajo.

As has been seen, the verb endings for the infinitive of all Spanish verbs are: AR, ER, and IR. When these are removed from the infinitive what remains is the verb stem. The endings for the tenses are added onto the stem.

Examples of stems.
**Hablar: to speak. Stem: Habl.....
**Beber: to drink. Stem Beb....
**Escribir: to write. Stem Escrib....

**AR verbs**. The verb endings for the present tense of AR verbs (in the order 1st person singular, 2nd person singular, 3rd person singular, 1st person plural, 2nd person plural, and 3rd person plural) are: o, as, a, amos, áis, an.

**ER verbs**. With ER verbs the present tense endings are: o, es, e, emos, éis, en

**IR verbs**. With IR verbs the present endings are: o, es, e, imos, ís en

Examples

| Present | Hablar AR verb | Beber ER verb | Escribir IR verb |
|---|---|---|---|
| Yo | hablo | bebo | escribo |
| Tú | hablas | bebes | escribes |
| Él/Ella/Ud. | habla | bebe | escribe |
| Nosotros/as | hablamos | bebemos | escribimos |
| Vosotros/as | habláis | bebéis | escribís |
| Ellos/as/Uds. | hablan | beben | escriben |

# Chapter 5.
## The Imperfect Tense

The imperfect tense is a statement of something in the past that was in some sense continuing at the time being spoken of. The action went on for a while or was continuous in the past. What it does not do is to express one thing that occurred, specifically at one time, or just once.

In English the imperfect may expressed by using the past progressive, by '*used to*' followed by the infinitive, or by the past historic, or by '*would*' (see further below), with the sense of the imperfect being understood from the context. In Spanish there is a specific tense and the fact that there is no exact equivalent in English may lead some to think of the imperfect as being a missing English tense; but really it is a matter of the imperfect being expressed and understood in the different ways described.

Examples.
** He always read the paper....Siempre leía el periodico.
** She used to speak......Ella hablaba....
** The idea was not taking him by surprise ......La idea no le cogía de sorpresa
** While I was walking to work this morning....... Mientras caminaba al trabajo esta mañana
** My brother was sleeping when...............Mi hermano dormía cuando ..............
** He used to travel by train........Viajaba en tren

By way of comparison note that the following would **not** be the imperfect but the past historic (preterite): I overslept last night. He read the paper and then gave it to me. Yesterday I travelled to work by train.

As mentioned above, in English the word "would", instead of indicating something conditional, may be used for the imperfect, and refer to circumstrances which were occuring in the past. In Spanish the conditional would **not** be used to express the idea of something continuous in the past. The imperfect would be used.

** At the foot of a barrier where the small lizards would creep....Al pie de un vallado por donde serpeaban las largatijas...

** That lady is the one who would send me fruit when I was sick.....Aquella señora es la que me mandaba frutas cuando you estaba enfermo

Further examples of the imperfect will be found in Chapter 6 dealing with the Preterite or Past Historic, where some comparisions of both tenses are provided.

The Spanish imperfect tense is one of the easiest conjugations to learn as will now be seen.

**AR Verbs:** With AR verbs the endings in the imperfect are as follows:
aba, abas, aba, ábamos, abais, aban.

**ER and IR verbs**. ER and IR verbs each have the same imperfect tense endings which are: ía, ías, ía, íamos, íais, ían.

Examples.

| Imperfect | Hablar AR verb | Beber ER verb | Escribir IR verb |
|---|---|---|---|
| Yo | hablaba | bebía | escribía |
| Tú | hablabas | bebías | escribías |
| Él/Ella/Ud. | hablaba | bebía | escribía |
| Nosotros/as | hablábamos | bebíamos | escribíamos |
| Vosotros/as | hablabais | bebíais | escribías |
| Ellos/as/Uds. | hablaban. | bebían | escribían |

Note that the imperfect tense is completely regular for **all** Spanish verbs except for Ir (to go), Ver (to see) and Ser (to be).

The conjugations for these 3 verbs in the imperfect are as follows:-

| Imperfect | Ser (to be) | Ver (to see) | Ir (to go) |
|---|---|---|---|
| Yo | era | veía | iba |
| Tú | eras | veías | ibas |
| Él/Ella/Ud. | era | veía | iba |
| Nosotros/as | éramos | veíamos | íbamos |
| Vosotros/as | erais | veíais | ibais |
| Ellos/as/Uds. | eran | veían | iban |

# Chapter 6.
## The Preterite or Past Historic Tense.

The past historic tense is a statement of something that occurred just once. The tense is used to express an action which has been fully completed. This may be compared with the imperfect where the intention is to refer to an action which is in some way continuing.

Consider the following examples of use of both tenses.

### Preterite
** He read the paper yesterday...Leyó el periódico ayer
** She spoke to me about it.......Ella me habló de ello
** I walked to work today..Anduve a trabajar hoy
** I learned Spanish at school... Aprendí español en la escuela
** He travelled by train yesterday ... Viajó en tren ayer
** He turned around....Se volvió

### Imperfect
** We thought that you were in the garden.....Creíamos que estabas en el jardín.
** He was reading the paper when.... Leía el periodico cuando......
** She knew all the plants......Ella conocía todas las plantas.....
** He was an agreeable man.....Era un caballero muy agradable

### Imperfect and Preterite
** Aun cuando el escondrijo daba (imperfect) espacio bastante, la pareja no se desunió (preterite) al encontrarse alli. .....Even when the hiding place gave sufficient space, the couple did not separate on finding themselves there.
** Ni menos se desviaron (preterite) sus rostros, tan cercanos, que él sentía (imperfect) el aletear de mariposa de los párpados de ella, y el cosquilleo de sus pestañas curvas....Nor less did they turn aside their faces, so close that he felt the butterfly flutter of her eyelids and the tickling of her curved eyelashes.

The Spanish preterite tense is not quite as easy to learn as the imperfect but should not present any real difficulty.

**AR Verbs**: With AR verbs the endings in the preterite are as follows: ...é, ....aste, .....ó, ...amos, .....asteis, ....aron.

**ER and IR verbs**. Both ER and IR verbs have the same preterite tense endings which are as follows: ...í ....iste, .....ió, ....imos, .....isteis, ....ieron.

**Examples**

| Preterite | Hablar AR verb | Beber ER verb | Escribir IR verb |
|---|---|---|---|
| Yo | hablé | bebí | escribí |
| Tú | hablaste | bebiste | escribiste |
| Él/Ella/Ud. | habló | bebió | escribió |
| Nosotros/as | hablamos | bebimos | escribimos |
| Vosotros/as | hablasteis | bebisteis | escribisteis |
| Ellos/as/Uds. | hablaron | bebieron | escribieron |

# Chapter 7.
## The Future Tense.

The future tense expresses something that will occur in the future, something that is going to happen. He will read the paper. She will speak to you. They will write a letter. The future tense in Spanish is much the same as in English.

Examples:
** Leeré el periodico mañana. I will read the newspaper tomorrow.
** El año que viene venderemos la casa. Next year we will sell the house.
** Tomarás una cerveza? Will you have a beer?
** Las personas que viven en esta casa serán ricas. The persons who live in that house will be rich. (Here the future indicates conjecture)

The Spanish future tense is one of the easiest tenses to learn because the endings are the same for all three types of verbs: AR, ER, and IR.

The endings are as follows: ...é, ...ás, ...á ...emos, ...éis, ...án.
However the verb endings for the future tense (and also for the conditional tense) are not added to the verb stem as with other verbs, but are added to the infinitive.

## Examples

| Future | AR<br>Hablar | ER<br>Beber | IR<br>Escribir |
|---|---|---|---|
| Yo | hablaré | beberé | escribiré |
| Tú | hablarás | beberás | escribirás |
| Él/Ella/Ud. | hablará | beberá | escribirá |
| Nosotros/as | hablaremos | beberemos | escribiremos |
| Vosotros/as | hablaréis | beberéis | escribiréis |
| Ellos/as/Uds. | hablarán | beberán | escribirán |

## Verbs which are irregular in the future and conditional tenses

Fortunately the number of Spanish verbs which are irregular in the future tense is limited to just twelve and all are easy to learn. Moreover the irregularity does not relate to the endings for the future tense but to what would otherwise be the infinitive form to which they are attached. As will be seen from the following comprehensive list, the irregularities mostly consist of the dropping of the final vowel for some of the infinitives, or the replacement of the vowel with the letter d, and in only two cases, decir and hacer, does the stem change completely.

Exactly the same changes occur for the conditional tense and so in the following table both the future and the conditional are shown. For each verb just the conjugation for the first person singular (yo) is given. All the other persons have exactly the same variation to the infinitive stem.

| Infinitive | Future (yo) | Conditional (yo) |
| --- | --- | --- |
| Decir | dir-é | dir-ía |
| Poner | pondr-é | pondr-ía |
| Salir | saldr-é | saldr-ía |
| Valer | valdr-é | valdr-ía |
| Querer | querr-é | querr-ía |
| Tener | tendr-é | tendr-ía |
| Hacer | har-é | har-ía |
| Haber | habr-é | habr-ía |
| Poder | podr-é | podr-ía |
| Saber | sabr-é | sabr-ía |
| Caber | cabr-é | cabr-ía |
| Venir | vendr-é | vendr-ía |

# Chapter 8.
## The Conditional Tense

The conditional tense (in English, something that I, you, he etc. *would* do if ...) generally expresses the idea, as the word conditional suggests, of something that is not certain: it is subject to a condition. Accordingly the use of the conditional generally implies or uses the words 'if', or 'but', or 'however', or similar qualification, or some explanation that the action proposed by the verb may not occur.

Examples:
\*\* I would pass (conditional tense) the exams, if I could only find the energy to study more.
\*\* I would read (conditional tense) the paper if I knew where it is.
\*\* She would speak (conditional tense) to you, however she does not have time at the moment.

Also the conditional tense is often associated with the subjunctive: however this will be covered in a later chapter.

The conditional tense is especially easy to learn because it is so regular. The endings are as follows: ...ía, ....ías, ....ía, ...íamos, ...íais, ...ían; and these are simply added on to the infinitive.

Moreover just like the future tense, the endings are the same for all verbs types: ar, er and ir. Additionally, as has already been commented, the irregularities are confined to exactly the same 12 verbs as for the future tense. A table for these 12 has been set out in the chapter dealing with the future tense.

Examples of the conditional

| Conditional | Ar<br>hablar | Er<br>beber | Ir<br>escribir |
|---|---|---|---|
| Yo | hablaría | bebería | escribiría |
| Tú | hablarías | beberías | escribirías |
| Él/ella/Ud. | hablaría | bebería | escribiría |
| Nosotros/as | hablaríamos | beberíamos | escribiríamos |
| Vosotros/as | hablaríais | beberíais | escribiríais |
| Ellos/as/Uds. | hablarían | beberían | escribirían |

As mentioned above the conditional is used:-

(a) to describe something that would occur if some condition is fulfilled.
** My sister would buy a car, if she had the money.
** Mi hermana compraría un coche, si tuviese el dinero.

** If she had a car she would lend it to you
** Si ella tuviese un coche, se lo prestaría a Ud.

The above two examples are both 'if/conditional' sentences, as to which see Chapter 13.

(b) to indicate approximation or probability with regard to some matter in the past.
** It would have been two o'clock at night.
** Serían las dos de la noche.

** She would have been ill because......
** Ella estaría enferma porque.....

(c) to express a wish, request or desire.
** She would like a coffee.
** Ella desearía un café.

** I would like to buy the book
** Me gustaría comprar el libro.

Note: when using querer, it may often be more appropriate to employ the imperfect subjunctive 'iera' form. The subjunctive imperfect is sometimes used in place of the conditional. For example: 'I should like a coffee.' 'quisiera un café.' This would be considered to be a more courteous form of expression than saying 'I would like a coffee.'

(d) after a past tense followed by 'que' and expressing something, which, viewed from the past being spoken of, would be some time after that.
** I thought that you would write to me.
** Creía que me escribiría

** She said she would sell the book.
** Ella dijo que vendería el libro.

** He promised me that he would arrive tomorrow.
** Me prometió que llegaría mañana.

Such main clauses in a sentence of this type would be in the indicative and suggest saying, believing, knowing, affirming assuring, and other expressions of this nature.

The clause with the verb in the conditional may appear either before or after the clause with the verb in the indicative.

Compare the following sentences:-
1. He said that he would do it. Dijo que lo haría.
Note: past tense in main clause with the dependent conditional referring to what then would have been the future.

But
2. He says that he will do it. Dice que lo hará.
Note: present tense with the dependent clause referring to the future.

3. He says that he would not talk so much if he were in front of the judge.
Dice que no hablaría tanto si estuviese delante del juez.
Note: present tense introducing if/conditional clause with conditional and subjunctive.

Remember, as explained in relation to the imperfect tense, that although in English the conditional may sometimes be used to express the idea of something continuing in the past, in Spanish the imperfect would be used for this purpose and not the conditional.

## Chapter 9.
## Haber and the Compound Tenses.
## Also: Hay, Habia, other forms derived from the verb Haber.

**1.The Present-Perfect Tense: 2. The Pluperfect or Past-Perfect Tense. 3. The Preterite Perfect Tense. 4.The Future Perfect Tense. 5. The Conditional Perfect Tense. 6. The Present-Perfect Subjunctive Tense. 7. The Pluperfect Subjunctive Tense.**

There are seven compound tenses as listed above and, despite the word "compound", they all are in fact amongst the easiest tenses to learn. And with the exception of the two compound subjunctive forms, which admittedly require a little extra study, the compound haber tenses are also relatively easy to use in practice.

**Note 1.** All the compound tenses employ the auxillary verb Haber. Except for some purposes described below, this verb is always used, with the Past-Participle for the relevant activity, to form the required tense. Note also that the Past-Participle when conjugated with haber does not agree with its object (unlike an adjective). So, being part of the verb tense with haber the Past-Participle will always end with o.

**Note 2.** Haber is translated as 'to have'. However the verb haber does not mean the same as the verb Tener, which means 'to hold' or 'to have to' etc.; and haber cannot generally be used on its own as Tener can be.

**Note 3.** It will be recollected that the verb is described as the Past-Participle when it is in the form in which it is added to another verb to give an indication of the past. E.G. He has stopped. 'Stopped' is here the Past-Participle.

In Spanish the Past-Participle of a verb will generally end as follows:
Verbs ending in AR: ...ado. E.G. Hablado = Spoken
Verbs ending in ER:.....ido. E.G. Corrido = Run
Verbs ending in IR ......ido. E.G. Partido = Left/departed
In each case the final two letters are removed from the infinitive and the ado or ido as appropriate tacked on.

There are some irregular Past-Participles, but not many and those that there are should not cause any difficulty. In the 104 Fully Conjugated Spanish Verbs and in the 1001 Most Useful Spanish Verbs provided with this book, the Past-Participle is always shown together with the infinitive, so again they will be easy to pick up and learn.

The tenses for Haber are given in the examples following and once they have been learned they can be used with the Past-Participle of <u>any verb,</u> so a great addition to the verb skills commanded will be achieved just by the modest amount of study required to master them.

These then are the conjugations of the seven compound haber tenses:-

## 1. The Present-Perfect Tense.
He, Has, Ha, Hemos, Habéis, Han.
English equivalent: "I have + Past-Participle". The tense is used to talk about some occurrence in the past, either at some uncertain time, or which in may some way still be continuing or is not quite complete. "I have passed my exams". "I have worked here for the last two years."

Examples
** He vendido el coche. I have sold the car.
** Él ha perdido su sombrero. He has lost his hat
** Hemos comprado una casa. We have bought a house.

## 2. The Pluperfect or Past-Perfect Tense.
Había, Habías, Había, Habíamos, Habíais, Habían.
English equivalent: "I had etc. + Past-Participle". Use of this tense is the same as it would be in English. It describes something that had occurred before some other event in the past (the other event not necessarily being mentioned because it is perhaps known or assumed or has been expressed previously).

Examples
**Antes de recibir tu carta yo había vendido el coche. Before receiving your letter I had sold the car.
**Antes de llegar a su despacho él había perdido su sombrero. Before arriving at his office he had lost his hat.
**Yo había leido el libro antes de darselo a mi hermana. I had read the letter before giving it to my sister.

### 3. The Preterite Perfect Tense.
Hube, Hubiste, Hubo, Hubimos, Hubisteis, Hubieron.
English equivalent: "I had etc.+ Past-Participle". This tense is really quite close in meaning to the pluperfect tense above. Whilst the student ought to know the conjugations of this tense so as to be able to understand them should they be encountered, it is not really necessary to worry about employing them in speech because the pluperfect will always suffice and the preterite perfect would not often be used in conversation.

### 4. The Future Perfect Tense.
Habré, Habrás, Habrá, Habremos, Habréis, Habrán.
English equivalent:"Will have" "shall have"+ Past-Participle. The tense is used just as it would be in English to express something that will occur in the future, subsequent to some other occurrence that is anticipated. The tense may also refer to the probability as to something that occurred recently.

Examples
** Habré vendido el libro antes de las dos.  I will have sold the book before two o'clock.
** Habrá perdido su sombrero de nuevo. He will have lost his hat again.
** Supongo que habrán comprado una casa. I suppose that they will have bought a house.

### 5. The Conditional Perfect Tense.
Habría, Habrías, Habría, Habríamos, Habríais, Habrían.
English equivalent: "Would have." + Past-Participle.   The tense indicates what would have happened if some condition had been satisfied. "I would have sent you a present with this letter if only I had remembered it was your birthday before I sealed the envelope."

Examples
** Habría vendido el coche si no lo hubiera* perdido. I would have sold the car if I had not lost it.
** Él habría perdido su sombrero si ella no lo hubiera* encontrado. He would have lost his hat if she had not found it.
** Habríamos comprado una casa si hubieramos* tenido el dinero.  We would have bought a house if we had had the money.
(* This is the pluperfect subjunctive.)

31

## 6. The Present-Perfect Subjunctive Tense.

Haya, Hayas, Haya, Hayamos, Hayáis, Hayan.

English equivalent: There is no quite appropriate English equivalent to this tense because the subjunctive is so little used in English. The words "should have".. "may have"..."might have" + Past-Participle, are about the best translation that can be suggested, but these words are not always evident in English. The tense is more fully discussed in the chapter on the subjunctive.

Examples

** Temo que él haya vendido el coche. I fear that he may have sold the car.

** Dudo que él haya perdido su sombrero. I doubt that he might have lost his hat.

** Siento que ellos hayan comprado una casa. I am sorry that they have bought a house.

## 7. The Pluperfect (or Past-Perfect) Subjunctive Tense.

This tense has two forms.

Either: Hubiera, Hubieras, Hubiera, Hubiéramos, Hubierais, Hubieran.

Or: Hubiese, Hubieses, Hubiese, Hubiésemos, Hubieseis, Hubiesen.

English equivalent: As with the Present-Perfect subjunctive, there is no exact translation for this tense into English. "Might have " and "should have" + Past-Participle are again the nearest equivalents, but these are not to be regarded as close translations. More usually in English the simple pluperfect would be used where in Spanish the pluperfect subjunctive would be employed.

This tense is more fully discussed in the chapter on the subjunctive.

Examples

** Yo temía que él hubiera (hubiese) vendido el coche. I feared that he had sold the car.

** Ella dudaba que él hubiera (hubiese) perdido su sombrero. She doubted that he might have lost his hat.

** Él sentía que hubiéramos (hubiésemos) comprado una casa. He was sorry that we should have bought a house.

**Hay, Habia, and expressions derived from the verb Haber**

In addition to use as an auxillary verb, there are other forms derived from haber as follows:

1. Haber followed by de and an infinitive represents the following meanings: to have to, to be required to, to be to, etc.
Example: **Hemos de comer a las cuatro: We have to eat at four o'clock.

2.Haber used impersonally will mean: there is, there are, there were etc.
Examples
**Hay buenas noticias en el periodico: there are good news in the newspapers.
**Hay muchos huevos en la cocina?:...Are there many eggs in the kitchen?
**No hay nadie....: there is no-one....
**Habrá mucho sol este dia: there will be much sun today
**Había mucho sol ayer: there was much sun yesterday
**Habría ....t here would be.....
**Hubo........there was....
**Ha habido......there has been.........

3. Haber used impersonally when followed by que and an infinitive denotes necessity or obligation.
Examples:
** Hay que leer el libro: It is necessary to read the book
** Había que perdonarle: It was necessary to forgive him.
** Que hay que hacer?: What is to be done?

**Haber compound tenses illustrated with Hablar and Quejarse.**

As has been seen, the conjugations of haber are always the same and only the Past-Participles are different between the verbs with which it is used as an auxillary.

Once you have learned the tenses of haber and used them with the Past-Participle for any verb, then you will be able to conjugate the compound forms **for every verb** for which you have learned the Past-Participle. See examples following.

# Haber+ Hablar: to talk/to speak

| Verb infinitive | Participles | |
|---|---|---|
| Haber/hablar compound tenses | Hablar: hablado | |
| | | |
| **Present-Perfect** | **Present-Perfect subjunctive** | **Future Perfect** |
| yo he hablado | yo haya hablado | yo habré hablado |
| tú has hablado | tú hayas hablado | tú habrás hablado |
| él ha hablado | él haya hablado | él habrá hablado |
| nosotros hemos hablado | nosotros hayamos hablado | nosotros habremos hablado |
| vosotros habéis hablado | vosotros hayáis hablado | vosotros habréis hablado |
| ellos han hablado | ellos hayan hablado | ellos habrán hablado |
| | | |
| **Pluperfect** | **Pluperfect subjunctive 1** | **Conditional Perfect** |
| yo había hablado | yo hubiera hablado | yo habría hablado |
| tú habías hablado | tú hubieras hablado | tú habrías hablado |
| él había hablado | él hubiera hablado | él habría hablado |
| nosotros habíamos hablado | nosotros hubiéramos hablado | nosotros habríamos hablado |
| vosotros habíais hablado | vosotros hubierais hablado | vosotros habríais hablado |
| ellos habían hablado | ellos hubieran hablado | ellos habrían hablado |
| | | |
| **Preterite Perfect** | **Pluperfect-subjunctive 2** | |
| yo hube hablado | yo hubiese hablado | |
| tú hubiste hablado | tú hubieses hablado | |
| él hubo hablado | él hubiese hablado | |
| nosotros hubimos hablado | nosotros hubiésemos hablado | |
| vosotros hubisteis hablado | vosotros hubieseis hablado | |
| ellos hubieron hablado | ellos hubiesen hablado | |

## Haber/Quejarse: to complain

| Verb infinitive | Participles | |
|---|---|---|
| Haber/quejarse compound tenses | quejado, quejándose | |
| | | |
| **Present-Perfect** | **Present-Perfect subjunctive** | **Future Perfect** |
| me he quejado | me haya quejado | me habré quejado |
| te has quejado | te hayas quejado | te habrás quejado |
| se ha quejado | se haya quejado | se habrá quejado |
| nos hemos quejado | nos hayamos quejado | nos habremos quejado |
| os habéis quejado | os hayáis quejado | os habréis quejado |
| se han quejado | se hayan quejado | se habrán quejado |
| | | |
| **Pluperfect** | **Pluperfect subjunctive 1** | **Conditional Perfect** |
| me había quejado | me hubiera quejado | me habría quejado |
| te habías quejado | te hubieras quejado | te habrías quejado |
| se había quejado | se hubiera quejado | se habría quejado |
| nos habíamos quejado | nos hubiéramos quejado | nos habríamos quejado |
| os habíais quejado | os hubierais quejado | os habríais hablado |
| se habían quejado | se hubieran quejado | se habrían quejado |
| | | |
| **Preterite Perfect** | **Pluperfect-subjunctive 2** | |
| me hube quejado | me hubiese quejado | |
| te hubiste quejado | te hubieses quejado | |
| se hubo quejado | se hubiese quejado | |
| nos hubimos quejado | nos hubiésemos quejado | |
| os hubisteis quejado | os hubieseis quejado | |
| se hubieron quejado | se hubiesen quejado | |

# Chapter 10.
## The Progressive Tenses

The progressive tenses are formed using the verb estar and the Present-Participle of the relevant verb. The action described by the verb is in progress at the time being spoken of. It is not something which has been completed.

It will be recalled that the Present-Participle form of the verb in English is recognizable by having the letters ING at the end. Running, walking, talking etc.

In Spanish the Present-Participle of a verb will end as follows:
Verbs ending in AR: drop AR and add..."ando". E.G. Hablar...Hablando = Speaking
Verbs ending in ER: drop ER and add...."iendo". E.G. Correr...Corriendo = Running
Verbs ending in IR ..drop IR and add..."iendo". E.G. Partiendo = Leaving/departing

The Spanish progressive tenses then are similar to the English progressive tenses which also use the verb 'to be' together with the Present-Participle, which makes remembering the Spanish form easier; although it should perhaps be added that some English speakers are in the habit of using the Past-Participle with these tenses, saying for example "He was/is sat" (instead of "sitting"), or "They were/are stood" (instead of "standing"). However the use of the Past-Participle for the progressive tenses is of course inappropriate in English, as it would also be in Spanish.

Note 1: The above comments should not be confused with the fact that the Past-Participle may sometimes be used with the verb 'to be', not as part of the verb expressing the action, but as an adjective; and in these circumstances it will, like any adjective in Spanish, have to agree in gender and number with the noun which it modifies.

Example:
** The flowers are dead: Las flores están muertas.
But: **The flowers are dying: Las flores están muriendo.

Note 2: There are some irregular Present-Participles. For example: pedir - pidiendo,
leer - leyendo, decir - diciendo, oir - oyendo, ir - yendo. Accordingly it is best always to learn the participles (present and past) when learning the verb.

**The Present-Progressive** tense is formed by adding the Present-Participle of the verb for the relevant activity as a separate word after the verb estar in the present tense.

For example: I am running. (Estoy corriendo.) I am dancing. (Estoy bailando).

**The Past-Progressive** is formed by adding the Present-Participle of the verb for the relevant activity as a separate word after the verb estar in the imperfect tense. Clearly the Past-Progressive has much in common with the use of the imperfect generally; and it may sometimes be preferable to use the imperfect of the relevant verb instead of the Past-Progressive.

For example: I was running. (Estaba corriendo.) I was dancing. (Estaba bailando).

| Progressive tenses | Present-Progressive tense Correr | Past-Progressive tense Bailar |
|---|---|---|
| Yo | Estoy corriendo | Estaba bailando |
| Tú | Estás corriendo | Estabas bailando |
| Él/Ella/Ud. | Está corriendo | Estaba bailando |
| Nosotros/as | Estamos corriendo | Estábamos bailando |
| Vosotros/as | Estáis corriendo | Estabais bailando |
| Ellos/as/Uds. | Están corriendo | Estaban bailando |

Other tenses of Estar may also be used with the Present-Participle.
In the table below only first person singular (Yo) in each case are shown,
but of course the Present-Participle applies to all the persons.

| | |
|---|---|
| **Preterite** | Yo estuve bailando |
| **Future** | Yo estaré bailando |
| **Conditional** | Yo estaría bailando |

**Use of the progressive tenses**.

1.The progressive tenses in Spanish are used in more or less the same way as they would be in English, save that the the matter being spoken of is something **is** actually going on at that moment of speaking (Present-Progressive); or **was** actually going on at the moment being spoken of (Past-Progressive or preterite progressive); or will actually be going on in the future (future progressive); or would actually be going on (conditional progressive). So the tense is more deliberate than it would be in English where the progressive tenses are likely to be used in a less forceful way. Note also that the Spanish imperfect tense translates into English much as would the Spanish progressive past. IE I was....he was....etc.

2 Where a progressive tense is used, any object pronoun referred to by the verb will be tacked onto the end of the Present-Participle. EG Estoy comprandolo etc.

3. The Present-Progressive tense in Spanish would not be used to deal with some future event. For example in English one might say "I am driving home tomorrow". This use of the Present-Progressive tense would not be appropriate in Spanish where the present or future tense would employed instead.  "I will drive home tomorrow"

4. As the Present-Participle used in a progressive tense is part of the verb, it does not have to agree in number or gender with the subject noun.

# Chapter 11.
## The Passive Voice

The passive voice is the use of a verb construction that avoids making the subject of the sentence the agent of the activity described, or that avoids having any clear subject.

Examples
** "The car was crashed by the drunken driver". In this sentence the car is the subject of the sentence but was not reponsible for the crash which was caused by the driver. By way of contrast consider the sentence in the active form. "The drunken driver crashed the car." Here the driver is the subject and carried out the action.

** "Fresh fish sold here". The sentence does not specify by whom the fish is sold.

** "Here they sell fresh fish" Again it is left unspecified who "they" may be.

** "It is not permitted to walk on the grass". The sentence does not make clear who may have made the order not to walk on the grass.

Before the different forms of the passive in Spanish are discussed it should be noted that, especially in spoken Spanish, the passive construction is avoided where practical, although where appropriate it will be used.

### The Passive Using the verb Ser
One form of the passive voice in Spanish is the use of the verb Ser plus the Past-Participle of the relevant verb. The Past-Participle has already been discussed in relation to the compound tenses and so need not be further explained here. However it must be remembered that when the Past-Participle is used with Ser in the passive voice, it is like an adjective and must agree both as to number and as to gender with the subject of the sentence. (NB It will be recalled that the Past-Participle, when used not with Ser but in a compound tense with Haber, is always the simple Past-Participle and is **not** made to agree with the subject.)

Examples
** El pescado fue cocinado. The fish was cooked.

** Los huevos fueron cocinados. The eggs were cooked.
** Las patadas fueron cocinadas. The potatoes were cooked.

The agent or person responsible for the action in the passive sentence may be introduced after the verb, by the word 'por' followed the name of the agent.

Examples
** El pescado fue cocinado por el cocinero. The fish was cooked by the cook.
** Los huevos fueron cocinados por el cocinero. The eggs were cooked by the cook.
** Las patadas fueron cocinadas por el cocinero. The potatoes were cooked by the cook.

However bear in mind that it is preferable in Spanish to use the active voice if possible. Accordingly the above sentences could be better expressed as:
** El cocinero cocinó el pescado. etc.

**The Passive using the reflexive form Se.**
A futher use of the passive voice requires a reflexive form. The verb dealing with the action is expressed in the third person, either single or plural, preceded by the reflexive 'Se'.

Examples:
** Fresh fish sold here. Aqui se vende pescado fresco.
This is literally to say: 'Here fresh fish sells itself'. Of course it is understood that fresh fish does not really sell itself, and that it is sold by persons unidentified in the sentence.

** Se escribirán muchos libros. Many books will be written.
** Se pegó al muchacho. The boy was beaten.

Note that where the action is done to a human it will be necessary to use the "a" to make it clear that the person concerned did not do the thing to himself. For example: "Se pegó el muchacho" would mean that the boy beat himself.

# Chapter 12.
## The Subjunctive Mood.
## When and how to use the subjunctive.

The subjunctive can be difficult to grasp when starting to learn Spanish, because it is a mood which is not much used, if at all, in English. Nonetheless the subjunctive form is in common use in in the Spanish language, and whilst an English speaker who does not use the subjunctive is unlikely to be seriously misunderstood when trying to express a relatively simple matter, to be able to speak good Spanish it is important to master the subjunctive.

The first point to note is that the subjunctive is mostly used only in dependent or subordinate clauses (unless used in imperative type sentences and expressions, which are dealt with in a later chapter). Accordingly (except with if/conditional clauses) the verb for the main clause in a sentence with a subjunctive will be in the indicative. The main clause in a sentence is that which expresses the main statement upon which any other clauses are dependant.

Example: ** 'I will come (main clause), though it may rain' (dependant clause with subjunctive).

N.B. The dependant clause may of course appear before the main clause. Example: ** 'Though it may rain, I will come.'

Secondly, the subjunctive does not express anything which is certain, or factual. Its use is to indicate doubt or desire, hope, or a possiblity etc. The subjunctive then is likely to be seen in sentences or clauses that are dependant on some other sentence that has shown that there is uncertainty, desire, a demand, etc.

The following sentences provide examples of the types of expressions that would indicate use of the subjunctive mood.

** Anxiety/Distress: I fear that he is unwell. I regret that he may not be able to come.
** Desire/Hope: I hope you have passed the exam. I hope that you tidy your room.
** Demand/Prohibition: We insist that you stop. He demands that you surrender.

** Uncertainty/Possibility: Perhaps she missed the train. It is possible that he has the book.
** Doubt. I doubt that he will keep his word.
** Negation: It is doubtful that the train is on time.


## The different forms of the subjunctive.

The subjunctives tenses are as follows:
The present subjunctive.
The imperfect subjunctive (which has two forms).
The perfect subjunctive.
The pluperfect subjunctive.
There is also a future subjunctive, but it is archaic and if encountered should be ignored.

## The Present Subjunctive.

The endings for the present subjunctive are as follows:
AR verbs: ...e, ...es, ...e, ...emos, ...éis, ...en.
ER and IR verbs: ...a, ...as, ...a, ...amos, ...áis, ...an.

Examples of the present subjunctive.

| Present Subjunctive | AR verb Hablar | ER verb Beber | IR verb Escribir |
|---|---|---|---|
| Yo | hable | beba | escriba |
| Tú | hables | bebas | escribas |
| Él/Ella/Ud. | hable | beba | escriba |
| Nosotros/as | hablemos | bebamos | escribamos |
| Vosotros/as | habléis | bebáis | escribáis |
| Ellos/as/Uds. | hablen | beban | escriban |

Nearly always, but not in every case, irregular or stem changing verbs in the present subjunctive have the same stem as the verb in the first person present indicative. So when trying to recollect the present subjunctive it may be helpful to recall what the present indicative tense would be for Yo. Whether this is regular or irregular the same stem is generally used to add the endings for the present subjunctive.

The verbs Hablar, Beber and Escribir, in the table above are all regular, but now consider three irregular verbs: Estar, Venir and Valer.

| Present Subjunctive | AR verb Estar | ER verb Valer | IR verb Venir |
|---|---|---|---|
| Yo | esté | valga | venga |
| Tú | estés | valgas | vengas |
| Él/Ella/Ud. | esté | valga | venga |
| Nosotros/as | estemos | valgamos | vengamos |
| Vosotros/as | estéis | valgáis | vengáis |
| Ellos/as/Uds. | estén | valgan | vengan |

## The Imperfect Subjunctive

The verb conjugations for the imperfect subjunctive are very easy to learn. The tense has two forms, either of which may generally be used. The endings for each are shown in the following table.

| Imperfect subjunctive | AR Verbs ...ra etc. | ER& IR Verbs ...ra etc | AR Verbs ...se etc. | ER& IR Verbs ...se etc. |
|---|---|---|---|---|
| Yo | -ara | -iera | -ase | -iese |
| Tú | -aras | -ieras | -ases | -ieses |
| Él/Ella/Ud. | -ara | -iera | -ase | -iese |
| Nosotros/as | -áramos | -iéramos | -ásemos | -iésemos |
| Vosotros/as | -arais | -ierais | -aseis | -iesies |
| Ellos/as/Uds. | -aran | -ieran | -asen | -iesen |

The memory trick for imperfect subjunctive is to take the third person plural (Ellos) of the preterite tense of the verb, removing the ending (which will be ARON for AR verbs and IERON for ER and IR verbs) and then applying the endings given above. This preterite rule for the formation of the imperfect subjunctive will be correct for all verbs, regardless as to whether the preterite is regular or irregular. This is why the imperfect subjunctive forms are easy to learn.

Note: The letters 'j', 'y' and 'ch' include the sound 'i' for this imperfect subjunctive rule so when these letters are left after removing the preterite ending, the 'i' in 'iera' and 'iese' is not used. The 'i' is already reflected in the j or y or ch. E.G. 'Leyeron' - 'leyesen' : 'Dijeron' - 'Dijesen': 'Hincheron' - 'Hinchesen'.

## The Compound Subjunctive Tenses

The compound tenses have already been discussed and it will be recalled that the auxillary verb used for them is Haber. It is always used with the Past-Participle ('Past-P') for the verb which it accompanies. There are two compound subjunctive tenses: the Perfect Subjunctive and the Pluperfect Subjunctive, the latter having two forms. Both are easy to remember due to their regular format.

### The Perfect Subjunctive.

| Perfect Subjunctive | Haber plus Past-Participle:Haya etc. |
|---|---|
| Yo | haya + Past-P |
| Tú | hayas + Past-P |
| Él/Ella/Ud. | haya + Past-P |
| Nosotros/as | hayamos + Past-P |
| Vosotros/as | hayáis + Past-P |
| Ellos/as/Uds. | hayan + Past-P |

### The Pluperfect Subjunctive. The two forms.

| Pluperfect Subjunctive | Haber plus Past-Participle: IERA etc. | Haber plus Past-Participle: IESE etc. |
|---|---|---|
| Yo | hubiera + Past-P | hubiese + Past-P |
| Tú | hubieras + Past-P | hubieses + Past-P |
| Él/Ella/Ud. | hubiera + Past-P | hubiese + Past-P |
| Nosotros/as | hubiéramos + Past-P | hubiésemos + Past-P |
| Vosotros/as | hubierais + Past-P | hubieseis + Past-P |
| Ellos/as/Uds. | hubieran + Past-P | hubiesen + Past-P |

### Circumstances in which the subjunctive would be used

1. Where the main clause indicates a request, an order, a prohibition etc.
Examples
** He tells me to come. Me dice que yo venga.
** I forbid them to dance. Prohibo que bailen.

44

** His mother has not allowed him to drink wine. Su madre no ha permitido que él bebiese vino.

2. Where the main clause indicates doubt, fear etc.
Examples
** I doubt that my brother will keep (may keep) his word. Dudo que mi hermano cumpla con su palabra.
** I fear that my father may speak to him about the matter. Temo que mi padre le hable del asunto.
** I am afraid the the teacher may not come. Temo que el profesor no venga.

3.Where the main clause indicates sorrow, joy, grief, surprise or other emotion.
Examples
** I am sorry that you should have troubled yourself. Siento que Ud se haya molestado.
** I am delighted that you have arrived. Me alegro que haya Ud llegado.
** I am glad that his exam has gone well. Celebro que le haya salido tan bien su examen.

4. Where the dependant clause begins with a conjunction, or a conjunctive expression and there is some uncertainty suggested. Typical conjunctions to look out for are: aunque, although, though: antes que, before: cuando, when: con tal que, on condition that: para que, in order that: como si, as if: por más que, however: sin que, without: dado que, provided that: á menos que, unless: puesto que, provided that: a fin que, in order: de modo que, so that: en caso de que, in case that.

Examples.
** I shall leave tomorrow though it may rain. Saldré mañana aunque llueva.
** I will not lend you my car unless you promise me to return it tomorrow. No le prestaré mi coche, á menos que me prometa devolverlo mañana.
** Whatever you may do, I will not forgive you. No te perdonaré, por más que hagas.

5. Where the dependant clause begins with a relative pronoun and there is some uncertainty suggested or implicit.
Examples.

** I want a teacher who speaks French. Quiero una profesora que hable francés.

** Show me a road that leads to Madrid. Enseñeme Ud un camino que salga para Madrid.

** If you want a drink that has no alcohol, I will supply it to you. Si Ud. quiere una bebida que no tenga alcohol, yo se la proporcionaré.

6. Where the main clause indicates a question or a denial/negative regarding the substance of the dependant clause.
Examples.

** Is there anyone who believes it? Hay alguien que lo crea?

** Do I say he is right? Digo yo que él tenga razon?

** Do you believe that they have arrived? Cree Ud que hayan llegado?

7. Where the main verb is impersonal and no certainty is indicated or implied.
Examples.

** It is right that he should know it. Es justo que lo sepa

** It may be that they know it. Puede ser que lo sepan.

** It is important that they should arrive on time. Importa que lleguen á tiempo.

8. The subjunctive may be used in a main clause for various declarations and expressions.
Examples.

**Long live Spain. Viva España

**Let no one go out. Que no salga nadie.

**God be with you. Vaya con Dios.

**I hope he comes soon. Ojalá venga pronto.

## Which tense of the subjunctive should be used and when?
The answer to this will depend upon:-
a) the tense of the verb in the main clause
b) the time of the matter referred to in the dependant subjunctive clause.

The following table sets out typical circumstances in which each form of subjunctive would be appropriate assuming that the factors exist, as described above, which require the use of the subjunctive (other than in 'If/Conditional clauses which are dealt with in Chapter 13). Examples of each are set out below the table.

| Main clause tense | Time of action referred to in dependant clause | Subjunctive to be used if subj. circs exist | Examples |
|---|---|---|---|
| Present indicative | Same time or later than main verb. | Present Subj. | **1.** below |
| Future indicative | In the future. | Present Subj. | **2.** below |
| A past tense | At same time or later as main verb | Imperfect Subj | **3.** below |
| Present indicative | Before time of main verb | Imperfect Subj | **4.** below |
| Future indicative | Before time of main verb. | Perfect Subj. | **5.** below |
| Present indicative | In the (perfect tense) past | Perfect Subj. | **6.** below |
| A past tense | Earlier than time of main verb | Pluperfect Subj. | **7.** below |

**Examples: 1.**
** Él prefiere que yo venga. He prefers that I should come.
** Siento que él no viva en la ciudad. I am sorry that he does not live in the town.
** Sugiero que duermas ahora. I suggest that you sleep now.

**Examples: 2.**
** Me dirá lo que escriban. He will tell me what they may write.
** Comeré lo que ella cocine. I will eat what she cooks.
** Terminaré este trabajo mañana si no vengan visitas. I will finish this work tomorrow, if no visitors come.

**Examples: 3.**
** Me extrañaba que no supieran cocinar. I was surprised that they did not know how to cook.
** Yo esperaba que ella cocinara. I expected that she should cook.
** Le dije al nino que se callase. I told the child to keep quiet.

**Examples: 4.**

** Temo que tuvieran que esperar un rato. I am afraid that they had to wait a while.

** Dudo que ella quisiera salir hoy. I doubt that she wanted to go out today.

** Parece imposible que el muchacho durmiera tanto. It seems impossible that the boy slept so much.

**Examples: 5.**

** Terminaré el trabajo cuando él haya pagado el dinero. I will finish the work when he has paid the money.

** Beberá cuando él haya comido. He will drink when he has eaten.

** Llegarán después de que hayan comprado un coche. They will arrive after they have bought a car.

**Examples: 6.**

** Dudo que él haya empezado su trabajo. I doubt that he has begun his work.

** Espero que ella haya dormido todo el dia. I expect that she has slept all day.

** Es un milagro que haya aprobado el examen. It is a miracle that he has passed the exam.

**Examples: 7.**

** Ella dudaba que él hubiera andado hasta la iglesia. She doubted that he had walked to the church.

** Ella esperaba que él hubiera mentido. She expected that he had lied.

** Parecía impossible que él no hubiera llegado. It seemed impossible that he had not arrived.

# Chapter 13.
## The Subjunctive and If/Conditional sentences.

If/Conditional sentences are those which contain both:

(a) An 'If-Condition' clause. This is a clause with a statement as to a condition. E.G. 'If I were you'. 'Si yo fuese Ud.'. ('If I were you', is incidentally, one of the few remaining uses of the subjunctive in English). Although we may call this clause the If-Condition clause, the verb in this clause will not be the conditional, but the subjunctive.
And
(b) A 'Would-Conclusion' clause. This is a clause with a statement as to what would occur if the condition set out in the If-Condition clause were to be satisfied. EG. 'I would buy the book'. 'Compraría el libro'. The verb in this Would-Conclusion clause will be in the conditional.

** If I were you I would buy the book. Si yo fuese Ud. compraría el libro.

Of course the above clauses may appear in either order. I.E. The If-Condition clause followed by the Would-Conclusion clause, or vice versa.

Although the If-Condition clause may frequently be commenced by if/si, other expressions such as 'aunque' may be used or implied.

Further examples of If/Conditional sentences:

** If I had time I would go to his house. Si yo tuviese tiempo, iría a su casa.
** I would not park the car here, if I were you. No aparcaría el coche aqui, si yo fuera Ud.
** If I had seen him, I would have asked him. Si lo hubiera visto, se lo habría preguntado.
** Even though he knew it, he would not have said it. Aunque lo supiera, no lo habría dicho.
** If I had given him money, he would have brought a new car. Si yo le hubiese dado dinero, él habría comprado un coche nuevo.

## Which form of the subjunctive should be used in the If-Condition clause?

In general, as has previously been seen, either of the 2 forms of the imperfect subjunctive may be used, each generally being equal to the other. However the imperfect subjunctive forms ending in ARA etc. and IERA etc. (but not ASE etc. or IESE etc.) can be and often are used instead of the conditional.

Moreover as will be clear, the ideas that may be indicated by 'I/he etc. would' and 'I/he etc. should' run fairly close in some matters. For example, as explained earlier, instead of saying 'I would like a coffee' it is more usual both in English and in Spanish to say 'I should like a coffee.' 'Quisiera un café'.

For this reason the ARA and IERA forms of the imperfect subjunctive may be used in place of the conditional tense in the Would-Conclusion clause of an If/Conditional sentence (but never the ASE or IESE forms).

However the use of the same form of the subjunctive in both the If-Condition clause and the Would-Conclusion clause is avoided. So if the ARA or IERA form is used in the If-Condition clause then the usual conditional tense should be used in the Would-Conclusion clause. The following examples should make this clear.

| If-Condition Clause | Would-Conclusion Clause |
|---|---|
| If I had time, | I would do it. |
| Si tuviese tiempo, | yo lo haría. |
| Si tuviera tiempo, | yo lo haría. |
| Si tuviese tiempo, | yo lo hiciera. |

# Chapter 14.
## The Imperative.
## When and how to use the imperative.
## Also: The imperative and object pronouns.

The imperative, like the subjunctive, is called a mood. It does not describe something that is factual or certain, but rather something which the speaker wants another person to do. The imperative is what is used when a command is given. For example: Do this! Do that! Stop that at once! Write this down! Bring me the book! Get up! Go to sleep! Do not snore! Do not run! Etc.

Note that there is no imperative form for the first person singular (Yo) because a command would be given to someone else and not to oneself. Even when telling oneself to do something it will be as though someone else is speaking. Accordingly no 'Yo' imperative form exists. However the imperative does exist for the first person plural (nosotros) because it is possible to address oneselves in the imperative as a group: Let us stop. Let us start. Also obviously, since the imperative is only addressed directly to someone, for the third persons singular and plural only the Ud. and Uds. forms exist.

The regular imperative forms for verbs ending in AR, ER, and IR are as follows:

| Imperative | Ar: Andar | Er: Beber | Ir: Escribir |
|---|---|---|---|
| tú | anda<br>no andes | bebe<br>no bebas | escribe<br>no escribas |
| Ud. | ande<br>no ande | beba<br>no beba | escriba<br>no escriba |
| nosotros | andemos<br>no andemos | bebamos<br>no bebamos | escribamos<br>no escribamos |
| vosotros | andad<br>no andéis | bebed<br>no bebáis | escribid<br>no escribáis |
| Uds. | anden<br>no anden | beban<br>no beban | escriban<br>no escriban |

# Memory points and Notes.

### Second person singular (Tú)
1.Positive commands:
This is formed just by dropping the S from the Tú form of the present indicative.

2. Negative commands:
This is formed by borrowing from the Tú form in the present subjunctive.

3. Reflexive verbs: see below.

### Third person singular (Ud.)
1. Positive and negative commands are both formed by borrowing from the Ud form in the present subjunctive.

2. Reflexive verbs: see below.

### First person plural (Nosotros)
1.Positive and negative commands are both formed by borrowing from the Nosotros form in the present subjunctive.

2. Reflexive verbs: see below.

### Second person plural (Vosotros)
1.Positive commands:
This is formed just by dropping the R from the infinitive of the verb and adding a D.

2. Negative commands:
This is formed by borrowing from the vosotros form in the present subjunctive.

3. Reflexive verbs: see below.

### Third person plural (Uds)
1. Positive and negative commands are both formed by borrowing from the Uds form in the present subjunctive. This of course is the same as adding N on to the end of the singular imperative Ud form.

2. Reflexive verbs: see below.

**Reflexive imperative forms.**
Spanish, like some other languages, often employs reflexive verbs and this being the case, the form of the imperative, as might be guessed, changes slightly where the verb is reflexive.

The regular imperative forms for reflexive verbs ending in AR, ER, and IR (with examples: Peinarse:to comb one's hair. Meterse: to go/to enter into. Aburrirse: to be bored.) are as follows:

| Imperative | Ar: Peinarse | Er: Meterse | Ir: Aburrirse |
|---|---|---|---|
| tú | péinate: no te peines | métete: no te metas | abúrrete: no te aburras |
| Ud. | péinese: no péinese | métase: no métase | abúrrase: no abúrrase |
| nosotros | peinémonos: no peinémonos | metámonos: no metámonos | aburrámonos: no nos aburramos |
| vosotros | peinaos: no os peinéis | meteos: no os metáis | aburríos: no os aburráis |
| Uds. | péinense: no péinense | métanse: no métanse | abúrranse: no abúrranse |

**Memory points and Notes.**
1. Second person singular (Tú) reflexive form
Positive command:- The reflexive TE is added to the end of the verb.
Example:- Comb your hair. Péinate. Note that the accent is shown over the first syllable to show that the stress remains as it would do if the TE were separated from the verb.
Negative command:- The reflexive TE appears before the verb.
Example:- No te peines. Note: no need here for an accent because it is clear that the stress falls on the first syllable.

2. Third person singular (Ud.) reflexive form:
Positive command:- The reflexive SE is just added on the end of the verb.
Example: Péinese

Negative commands: Generally the reflexive SE remains at the end of the verb.
Example: No péinese
However there are some exceptions and sometimes the reflexive SE appears in front of the verb. Example: No se lave.

3. First person plural (Nosotros) reflexive form
Positive command: The final S is dropped and the reflexive is then added on the end of the verb.
Example: Peinémonos
Negative commands: Generally the same as the positive command with No appearing before the verb.
Example: No peinémonos
However there are some exceptions and sometimes the reflexive Nos appears in front of the verb. Example: No nos lavémos.

4. Second person plural (Vosotros) reflexive form
Positive command: The final D is dropped and the reflexive OS is added to the end of the verb.
Example:- Comb your hair. Peinaos.
Negative command: The reflexive OS appears before the verb.
Example: No os peinéis.

5. Third person plural (Uds) reflexive form
Positive command:- The reflexive SE is just added on the end of the verb.
Example: Péinense
Negative commands: Generally the reflexive SE remains at the end of the verb.
Example: No péinense
However there are some exceptions and sometimes the reflexive SE appears in front of the verb. Example: No se laven.

**The imperative and object pronouns.**
Where the imperative command is positive the object pronoun or pronouns are tacked onto the end of the verb. Where there are two or more pronouns they should appear in the following order: Reflexive pronoun, indirect pronoun, direct pronoun.
Examples.

| | |
|---|---|
| ** Throw it! (Tú) Tíralo! | Throw it to me! (Tú) Tíramelo! |
| ** Sell it! (Tú) Véndelo! | Sell it to him! (Tú) Véndeselo! |

** Give me it! (Tú) Démelo!     Tell me it! (Ud.) Dígamelo!
** Learn it! (Ud.) Apréndalo!     Forget it! (Ud.) Olvídelo

Where the imperative is in the negative, the object pronouns are placed in front of the verb. Again where there are two or more pronouns they should appear in the following order: Reflexive pronoun, indirect pronoun, direct pronoun.
Examples.
** Do not throw it! (Tú) No lo tíres!
** Do not throw it to me! (Tú) No me lo tíres!
** Do not sell it! (Tú) No lo véndas!
** Do not sell it to him! (Tú) No se lo véndas!
** Do not give me it! (Tú) No me lo des!
** Do not tell me it! (Ud.) No me lo digas!
** Do not learn it! (Ud.) No lo apréndas!
** Do not forget it! (Ud.) No lo olvides!


The circumstances in which the imperative should be used are straightforward, but the variations can be a trifle fiddly. Here then, for those in a hurry, is an easy way to deal with commands: turn them into polite requests. Instead of saying 'do this/do that', say 'please do this/do that'. The Spanish for 'please' is ((Tú) 'Hazme el favor de ......'; or (Ud.) 'Hagame el favor de...'

'Haz' and 'Haga' are the Tú and Ud. imperative forms for Hacer (to do). These can be used with an infinitive to request the matter desired.
Examples: 'Hazme el favor de abrir la puerta'. (Please open the door); or 'Hagame el favor de abrir la puerta'.

# Chapter 15.
## Spanish verbs and the preposition 'a' before a specific person etc.

In Spanish the preposition 'a' is in many cases inserted in the sentence with the verb in circumstances where this would not occur in English.

The basic rule is that if the direct object of the sentence is a specific person or some item treated as though it were a person, such as the family dog that is treated as one of the family, then the preposition 'a' is inserted before the direct object.

For example:
** El padre ama a su hijo. The father loves his son.
** La chica quiere a su perro. The girl loves her dog.

The following then are the main circumstances in which the preposition 'a' would be used:

1. Where the direct object is a noun being a definite person or personified object.
Examples.
** El maestro busca a su alumno. The teacher looks for his pupil.
** El abogado representa a su cliente. The lawyer represented his client.
** No vio a su tío. He did not see his uncle.

2. Before the proper name of things, *except* where the definite article is part of the name (e.g. *El* Prado)
Examples
** Él quiere ver a España. He wants to see Spain.
** *But*: Quiero visitar el Prado. I want to visit the Prado.

3. The preposition 'a' would **not** be used:
(a) before a common noun
Examples
** Me estrellé mi coche. I crashed my car.
** Quemó la cena. He burned the supper.

(b) Before a noun for a person in an indefinite sense:
Example
** I need a teacher. Necesito un profesor.
** *But*: He found his teacher. Encontró a su profesor.

4. The 'a' will also be used to avoid ambiguity in a sentence where both the subject and the direct object are nouns for things.
Example
** Summer follows the spring. Verano sigue a la primavera.

5. Note:
(a) Querer means to want. 'Querer a' means to love.
So:
** I want a mother. Quiero un madre.
** I love my mother. Quiero a mi madre.

(b) Tener would not take the 'a'
** So: I have a mother. Tengo una madre.

# Chapter 16.
## Defective, Incomplete and Impersonal Verbs

There are a number of Spanish verbs which, as will be seen, are defective or incomplete in that not all the expected conjugations exist or, whilst they may exist, generally only the third person is used. There are other verbs which are only ever used impersonally (ie only in the third person).

**Impersonal Verbs**
(a) Impersonal verbs are those which for logical reasons are limited to the infinitives, the participles, and the third person of the relevant tense. Whilst in theory constructions with other conjugations might be possible, they are in fact avoided.
** Llover: to rain. Llueve: it rains.
** Nevar: to snow. Nieva: it snows.
** Amanecer: to dawn. Amanece: dawn breaks
** Atardecer: to to get dark. Atardece: dusk falls

(b) Hacer. In addition to it's use generally, hacer is used impersonally in the third person of the relevant tense, to refer to the temperature, the weather, and to time (in the sense of time past, ago etc.)
Examples
** Hace buen tiempo: The weather is good.
** Hace calor: It is hot.
** Ocurrió hace diez años; It happened ten years ago.

**Verbs used generally in just the third person.**
There are some verbs that (although possibly available in other conjugations) are like the impersonal verbs and are used generally in the third person.

The most obvious example of such verbs is gustar, which is used to mean to like, but which more accurately translates as: to please or to be pleasing to. For example: 'Me gusta la crema'. This would be translated as 'I like cream', but really means 'cream pleases me'.

Other similar verbs:
** Encantar: to delight, to enchant.
** Bastar: to be enough, to be sufficient.
** Importar: to matter, to be important.

** Doler: to hurt, to distress.

**Verbs which are incomplete**.
These are some verbs for which with some tenses or persons, there is no conjugation available. This at least is the theory but sometimes an example will be heard of a conjugation which 'does not exist'. In Spanish as in English, the rules are not always absolute, especially for an inventive speaker.

Examples
** Abolir: to abolish. Only used in those forms in which the i of the infinitive is retained; (this includes the participles).
** Soler: to be accustomed to, to be in the habit of. Not available in the future, the conditional, the future perfect, the conditional perfect, and the imperative.
** Costar: to cost. In theory only available in the third person and the participles.
** Antojarse: to covet, to long for. Only available in the third person and the Present-Participle.
** Atañer: to concern, to have to do with. Only available in the third person and the participles.

# Chapter 17.
## Distinction between the verbs Estar and Ser (to be)

Both these verbs translate into English as the verb "to be". However in Spanish these two verbs are each used for different purposes and neither can be used in place of the other. This distinction obviously would not occur in English where the single verb "to be" would be used.

A basic guide to bear in mind is that generally **ser** is used to indicate something permanent and **estar** to indicate something which may not last.

The table below indicates various circumstances for appropriate use of the verbs.

| | **Ser** examples | **Estar** examples |
|---|---|---|
| Progressive tenses | | Estoy escribiendo, Estaba escribiendo |
| Passive voice | El pescado fue cocinado | |
| Permanent personal details | Ella es inteligente El hombre es albañil | |
| Temporary personal details | | El muchacho está agotado |
| State of health | | La chica está enferma |
| Time of day | Son las dos | |
| Date | Hoy es domingo | |
| Ownership | El coche es mío | |
| Location | | Los platos sucios están sobre la mesa |
| Condition of things | | La cocina está sucia La catedral está abierta |
| Permanent condition of things | Las paredes de la catedral son de ladrillo | |

# Chapter 18.
## Some Spanish verbs having irregular or notable Past-Participles

The present and Past-Participles of all the verbs listed in this book are shown with those verbs. However here for convenience are some notable irregular forms of Past-Participles

| Verb infinitive | Past-Participle |
|---|---|
| Abrir, to open | abierto |
| Bendecir, to bless | bendito |
| Cubrir, to cover | cubierto |
| Decir, to say | dicho |
| Descubrir, to uncover | descubierto |
| Escribir, to write | escrito |
| Hacer, to make, to do | hecho |
| Imprimir, to print | impreso |
| Ir, to go | ido |
| Maldecir, to curse | maldito |
| Morir, to die | muerto |
| Poner, to put | puesto |
| Romper, to break | roto |
| Ver, to see | visto |
| Volver, to return, to turn | vuelto |

In verbs where the 'ido' of a Past-Participle follows the vowels a, e and o, the I of the ido will have an accent to show that it has the accent and is fully pronounced and that there is no diphthong.

| | |
|---|---|
| Creer, to believe | creído |
| Roer, to gnaw | roído |
| Leer, to read | leído |
| Traer, to bring | traído |

# Chapter 19.
## Examples of compound verbs derived from various irregular verbs

Compound verbs, that is verbs which are composed of some other verb plus a prefix, are conjugated in the same way as the verb without the prefix.

**Examples with irregular verbs:-**

**The following verbs are conjugated in the same way as Hacer:-**
Contrahacer, to copy, to counterfeit.
Deshacer, to undo.
Rehacer, to redo, to do again.

**The following verbs are conjugated in the same way as Poner:-**
Componer, to put together, to compose.
Deponer, to lay down, to remove, to depose.

**The following verb is conjugated in the same way as Salir:-**
Sobresalir, to project, to stand out

**The following verb is conjugated in the same way as Valer:-**
Equivaler, to be equal to, to rank the same as.

**The following verb is conjugated in the same way as Traer:-**
Retraer, to draw in, to retract.

**The following verbs are conjugated in the same way as Venir:-**
Convenir, to agree, to suit.
Revenir, to shrink, to come back.

**The following verbs are conjugated in the same way as Ver:-**
Prever, to foresee, to anticipate.
Rever, to see again, to review.

Note that some compound irregular verbs may have a different Past-Participle. Examples: Bendecir (bendito) and maldecir (maldito).

# Chapter 20.
## Reflexive Spanish Verbs

1. A reflexive verb is one where the object will be the same as the subject. In other words the person undertaking the action of the verb is the same as the object or person to whom the action of the verb occurs.

Examples.
** I shave myself. Yo me afeito.
** I stopped myself. Me detuve.
** They married: Se casaron.
** He undressed: Se desnudó.

2. The Spanish reflexive pronouns are as follows:
me (myself)
te (yourself)
se (him/her/(Ud) it's/self)
nos (ourselves)
os (yourselves)
se (them/(Uds) selves)

Example. Afeitarse: to shave oneself.

| Present tense | Perfect tense |
|---|---|
| me afeito | me he afeitado |
| te afeitas | te has afeitado |
| se afeita | se ha afeitado |
| nos afeitamos | nos hemos afeitado |
| os afeitáis | os habéis afeitado |
| se afeitan | se han afeitado |

3. In Spanish the use of the reflexive form is common, and will be normal wherever the action undertaken relates to the person undertaking it. This may be contrasted with English where the reflexive is not much used except where necessary to make quite clear that the action related to the object of the verb. "I hurt myself".

Bear in mind that the English 'myself'/ 'himself/ herself/themself' are often used not as a reflexive form but to reinforce or emphasise the identity of the person carrying out the action. For example 'I myself have read the book'. 'He drove the car himself'.

4. Spanish transitive verbs can generally be either reflexive or non reflexive.
Consider
** He shaved himself: Se afeitó.
** I shaved him. Le afeité
** He deceived me. Él me engañó
** I deceived myself . Me engañé a mí mismo.

5. However some Spanish verbs are used only reflexively.
** Alegrarse: to rejoice
** Atreverse a: to dare to

6. The third person reflexive would generally be used where possible instead of the passive form.
Examples:
** Fish is sold here. El pescado se vende aquí.
** How does one get to the bus station?  Cómo se llega a la estación de autobuses?
** How are eggs cooked? Cómo se cocinan los huevos?

7. Reciprocal Reflexives Verbs.
Verbs will be described as reciprocal reflexives, when they refer to two or more people acting one upon the other.
Examples:
** They deceived each other. Se engañan unos a otros.
** They bathed each other. Se bañaban unos a otros.

Unos a otros, or uno as otro, as appropriate, may be added as above for greater emphasis.

8. Some verbs have a different meaning when used as reflexives.
Examples
** Dormir: to sleep. Dormirse: to fall asleep.
** Ir: to go. Irse: to go away (in effect: to take oneself away)
** Sentir: to be sorry, to feel regret. Sentirse: to feel, to suffer hurt/unwell etc.

# Chapter 21.
## Orthographic, Euphonic and Stress changes in Spanish verbs.

**Note:**

**1.** The following comments as to the changes for various verbs are not intended to be learned, but to draw attention to what happens in the conjugation and to make the changes easier to appreciate. Read them to understand the verb types but not so as to learn as rules for conjugating them. 3. A fully conjugated example of all the verbs mentioned in this chapter can be found, in **Spanish Verb Perfect,** the companion volume to this book

**2. Key to abbreviations used below:**
O= Changes mostly Orthographic/Euphonic
S= Stem changes
M= Mixed changes/irregularities
Ú/Í= Stem U or stem I verb with stress changes

**3.** A fully conjugated example of all the verbs mentioned in this chapter can be found, in **Spanish Verb Perfect,** the companion volume to this book

**Orthographic and Euphonic changes**
Some types of verbs have changes for orthographic or euphonic reasons. The reason for the changes will generally be obvious, and a pattern may be evident.

**O-Bullir/Empeller**   Verbs in which the infinitives IR and ER are preceded by LL.
Changes: to Present-Participle, to preterite and imperfect subjunctive
The i in ie or io is dropped when they would have occured in the conjugation

**O-Bruñir/Tañer** - Verbs in which the infinitives IR and ER are preceded by Ñ.
Changes: to Present-Participle, preterite and imperfect subjunctive
The i in ie or io is dropped where it would otherwise have occured in the conjugation

**O-Henchir** Verbs in which the infinitive IR is preceded by CH.
Changes:  to Present-Participle, preterite and imperfect subjunctive

1) The i in ie or io is dropped when they would have occured in the conjugation.

2) Henchir is also a verb that has stem or root changes unconnected with the CHIR rule. Note that the e in the root changes to i in the present, present subjunctive and imperative.

**O-Rezar**_Verb with the ending zar.
Changes: to preterite, present subjunctive and imperative.
The z changes to c before e.

**O-Creer**_Verbs with an unaccented i between two vowels.
Change: the i becomes y.

**O-Tocar**_Verb with ending car.
Change: to preterite, present subjunctive and imperative.
C changes to qu before e.

**O-Pagar**_Verb ending in gar.
Changes: to preterite, present subjunctive and imperative.
G changes to gu before e.

**O-Averiguar**_Verb ending in guar.
Changes: to preterite, present subjunctive and imperative.
G changes to gü before e.

**O-Escoger**_Verb ending in ger.
Changes: to present, present subjunctive and imperative.
G changes to j before a or o.

**O-Dirigir**_Verb ending in gir.
Changes: to present, present subjunctive and imperative.
G changes to j before a or o.

**O-Distinguir**_Verb ending in guir.
Changes: to present, present subjunctive and imperative.
Gu changes to g before a or o.

**O-Delinquir**_Verb ending in quir,
Changes: to present, present subjunctive and imperative.
Qu changes to c before o and a.

**O-Vencer**__Verb with the ending cer **which is preceded by a consonant.**
Changes: to present, present subjunctive and imperative.
C changes to z before o and a.

**O-Esparcir**_Verb with the ending cir **which is preceded by a consonant.**
Changes: to present, present subjunctive and imperative.
C changes to z before o and a.

**O-Conocer**_Verb with the ending cer **which is preceded by a vowel**
Changes: to present, present subjunctive and imperative.
Z is inserted before the c when followed by a or o.

**O-Lucir**_Verb with the ending cir **which is preceded by a vowel**
Changes: to present, present subjunctive and imperative.
Z is inserted before the c when followed by a or o.

(Note: verbs ending in ducir, have further changes as to which see Producir below)

**M-Producir**_Verb ending in ducir.
Changes: to present, present subjunctive, imperfect subjunctive and imperative
1) Z is inserted before the c when followed by a or o.
2) Change the c of their stem to j in the preterite,
3) Irregular preterite endings as follows- ....je, ....jiste, ....jo, ....jimos, ....jisteis, ....jeron. The two imperfect subjunctive forms are always drawn from the preterite él form, as has been seen already, and so these also are irregular

**O-Instruir**_Verb ending in uir, in which the u is pronounced (but not those ending in guir, or güir in which the u is silent before the i)
Changes: to Present-Participle, preterite, present, present subjunctive, imperfect subjunctive and imperative
1) When accented or followed by a or o, the u becomes uy.
2) The i in terminations beginning with ie or io changes to y when unaccented (following the unaccented i between two vowels rule, as in **O. Creer**)

**2O-Argüir**_Verb ending in üir, in which the u is pronounced (but not those ending in guir, or güir in which the u is silent before the i
Changes: to present, present subjunctive, imperfect subjunctive and imperative
1) When accented or followed by a or o, the ü becomes uy.
2) The i in terminations beginning with ie or io changes to y when unaccented (following the unaccented i between two vowels rule, as in **8-O. Creer**)

**O-Caer**_Verb ending in aer.
Changes: to present, present subjunctive, imperfect subjunctive and imperative
1) Change the first person singular (yo) present tense to aigo, and become aiga etc. throughout the present subjunctive and imperative forms (except for the imperative positive tu and vosotros forms)
2) The i in terminations beginning with ie or io changes to y when unaccented (following the unaccented i between two vowels rule, as in **O- Creer.**)

Note: a number of verbs with aer endings, apart from taking aigo, are irregular in the preterite and related imperfect subjunctive forms and in these cases the y rule is not relevant. For example Traer)

**Stem/Stress Changing Verbs.**

**Stem or radical changing verbs.**
Further types of irregular verbs are those which undergo some change in their root or stem vowel, but which otherwise follow the regular rules for the endings. Regretably there are very many such verbs and moreover there is no easy criteria for indicating whether a verb will be stem changing just from its appearance. It is necessary to become acquainted with them by experience and usage.

With most of these stem changing verbs the changes will occur only in the present, the present subjunctive and the imperative forms. However there are also some which have stem changes in the preterite tense and consequently in the imperfect subjunctive forms which are drawn from the preterite. When you learnt the preterite you will easily know the imperfect subjunctive forms. In short: pay special attention to the present (which will generally give the key to the present subjunctive and the imperative) and the preterite (which always govern the imperfect subjunctive forms)

## Examples of verbs with stem changes

**S-Alentar/Acertar**_Verb ending in ar with stem vowel e.
Changes: to present, present subjunctive and imperative.
The e becomes ie when accented; but not where it is not accented.

**S-Perder/Entender**_Verb ending in er with stem vowel e.
Changes: to present, present subjunctive and imperative.
The e becomes ie when accented; but not where it is not accented.

**S-Aprobar/Acortar**_Verb ending in ar with stem vowel o.
Changes: to present, present subjunctive and imperative.
The stem vowel o becomes ue when accented; but not where it is not accented.

**S-Morder/Remover**_Verb ending in er with stem vowel o.
Changes: to present, present subjunctive and imperative.
The stem vowel o becomes ue when accented; but not where it is not accented.

**S-Oler**_Verb ending in er with stem vowel o. First letter is O.
Changes: to present, present subjunctive and imperative
1) O becomes ue when accented; but not where it is not accented.
2) H is inserted before the ue because Spanish words cannot begin with ue.

**S-Discernir/Cernir**_Verb ending in ir with stem vowel e.
Changes: to present, present subjunctive and imperative
E becomes ie when accented; but not where it is not accented.
Compare with **S-Sentir**

**S-Sentir/Advertir**_Verb ending in ir with stem vowel e.
Changes: to Present-Participle, present, preterite, present subjunctive, imperfect subjunctive and imperative.
1) E becomes ie when accented.
2) There is a further change in the preterite (and in the two imperfect subjunctive forms which are drawn from the preterite) and in the present subjunctive, the imperative and in the Present-Participle as follows. When the stem e is not accented, the e becomes i if the next

syllable contains a vowel other than just i on it's own (in other words if followed by two vowels or by a).
3) Compare with **S/Discernir**

**S-Servir/Competir**_Verb ending in ir where the stem vowel is e.
Changes: to Present-Participle, present, present subjunctive, imperfect subjunctive and imperative.
1) In the present, the present subjunctive, and the imperative, the e becomes i when the i is accented, or when followed by a.
2) In the preterite (and in the two imperfect subjunctive forms which are drawn from the preterite) and the Present-Participle: the e becomes i when the stem e is not accented and the next syllable contains a vowel other than just i on it's own (ie: if followed by two vowels).

**S-Adquirir/Inquirir**_Verb ending in ir with stem i
Changes: to present, present subjunctive and imperative
The i becomes ie when accented.

**S-Dormir/Morir**_Verb ending in ir where the stem vowel is o.
Changes: to participles, present, preterite, present subjunctive, imperfect subjunctive and imperative.
1) In the present, the present subjunctive, and the imperative, the o becomes ue when the o is accented, or when followed by a.
2) In the preterite (and in the two imperfect subjunctive forms which are drawn from the preterite) and the Present-Participle: the o becomes u when the stem o is not accented and the next syllable contains a vowel other than just i on it's own (ie: if followed by two vowels).

**S-Jugar**_Verb ending in gar where the stem vowel is u.
Changes: to present, preterite, present subjunctive and imperative
1) In the present, the present subjunctive, and the imperative, the u becomes ue when the u is accented, or when followed by a.
2) In the preterite: the present subjunctive, and the imperative, g becomes gu before e, following the rule in 7-O-Pagar.

**S-Reir/Freir**_Verb ending in eir (nb the stem vowel is e).
Changes: to Present-Participle, the present, preterite, present subjunctive, imperfect subjunctive and imperative
1) As with S-Servir, in the present, the present subjunctive, and the imperative, the e becomes i when the i is accented, or when followed by a.

2) As with **S-Servir**, in the preterite (and in the two imperfect subjunctive forms which are drawn from the preterite) and the Present-Participle: the e becomes i when the stem e is not accented and the next syllable contains a vowel other than just i on it's own (ie: if followed by two vowels).

3) In both 1) and 2), when the stem vowel e changes to i, the i of the terminations beginning with ie and io lose the i (ie: not a double i). Hence the Present-Participle is riendo (not reiendo or riiendo)

**S-Colegir/Elegir**_Verb ending in egir. (ie both gir and stem vowel e)
Changes: to Present-Participle, the present, preterite, present subjunctive, imperfect subjunctive and imperative
1) As with O-Dirigir the g changes to j before a or o.
2) As with S-Servir: in the present, the present subjunctive, and the imperative, the e becomes i when the i is accented, or when followed by a.
3) As with S-Servir: in the preterite (and in the two imperfect subjunctive forms which are drawn from the preterite) and the Present-Participle: the e becomes i when the stem e is not accented and the next syllable contains a vowel other than just i on its own (ie: if followed by two vowels.)


**Verbs with stress changes. (Verbs ending in uar or iar or which have u or i in their stem)**

Verbs which have two vowels next to one another, generally have the accent on the strong vowel; in other words on the a, e or o; the letters u and i being the weak vowels. However this is not invariable.

A number of verbs with the endings uar and iar, or which have u or i in their stem, may place the stress on the u or on the i as follows: namely in the yo, tu, él, and ellos forms (ie all persons other than nosotros and vosotros) of the present indicative, the present subjunctive, and the imperative. Typical verbs like this are:
**Ú/Í-Evaluar, Ú/Í-Ampliar, Ú/Í-Aullar, Ú/Í-Reunir, Ú/Í-Rehusar** (the h is silent so in effect eu), **Ú/Í-Airar, Ú/Í-Prohibir** (silent h so in effect oi).

**Verbs with mixed types of irregularities: i.e. those with conjugations derived from more than one of the variants described.**

Examples of verbs with orthographic or euphonic changes and verbs with Stem or radical changes. : **Henchir, Instruir, Argüir, Caer, Oler, Colegir, Elegir. Agorar, Almorzar, Avergonzar, Ceñir, Colgar, Empezar, Forzar, Regar, Seguir, Trocar,**

# Part Two: Mastering, Memorising and Recalling Spanish Verbs and Tenses

The chapters in this part of the book will show you how to learn Spanish verbs with both their meaning and in all their conjugations quickly and efficiently. Chapter 22 deals specifically with memory reinforcement techniques to be used at every stage in your learning of Spanish verbs. Chapter 23 details a learning method to be used with the techniques. Chapter 24 provides a number of valuable tips, and pointers to aid your memory of Spanish verb conjugations.

## Chapter 22
## Essential Memorizing Techniques For Spanish Verbs

As you begin to study individual verbs remember that despite the value of any rules or patterns for the verbs, the rules are not themselves the language. The use of a language by its speakers gives rise to the rules and not vice versa. It is more important to learn actual conjugations and the practical use of the verbs than any background technical comments as to their formation.

### The 9 Rs for Spanish verb learning
The learning of Spanish verbs, like any subject worth studying, must involve some effort and it is desirable that the efforts to be expended should secure the maximum results in proportion to the time spent. The following Memory 9 Rs will help you to achieve that.

**Reading Aloud:** Read aloud the conjugations of the verb to be learned verb.

**Reflection:** Think about the verb, its meaning, and any similarities with the conjugations of other verbs and any variations that it may have from the regular rules. Also reflect on the pronunciation of the verb conjugations. It is important always to try and speak with an authentic Spanish sound, but being aware of the correct pronunciation is also an aid to understanding and recalling the conjugations. As has been seen, many of the apparent irregularities of some verbs are due entirely to euphonic and spelling requirements. The basic sound of the particular conjugation may in fact follow the regular rule, but to achieve it, the spelling may vary from the regular. Additionally it is essential always know the right place for the accent, so as to express or understand the meaning intended.

**wRiting:** Writing down the verb and its conjugations is an aid to concentration and to re-enforcing your memory of them.

**Repetition**: Repeating the verb conjugations by frequent use, speaking, writing and re-reading. Simple repetition is desireable especially in the early stages of learning so as to begin to impose the verb and its conjugations on your memory.

### Other Repetition methods
**1.** Chant the verb conjugations to yourself frequently in the same way that probably you learned the times tables at school. In this way their use will more easily become second nature and should not be something that you have to think about..

**2.** Keep a notebook, both of the current selection of verbs that you are learning and of any other verbs that may be encountered and which might be useful. Alternatively make some flashcards (postcard size) with a selection of the weeks verbs to be studied; for example one verb and its conjugation set out on each side of the card. These have to be written out but this itself is a helpful aid to concentration and memory as has been seen. The cards or notebook can be carried around and taken out to study in spare moments during the day.

**Regular study**: A little and often is the way to study the verbs. A long period of study carried out infrequently will not yield the same results. Aim at studying your Spanish verbs for a short period every day; just 10 or 15 minutes a day will produce remarkable results within a short time.

**Reinforcement**: The verbs that you learn should be put to use as much as possible. Practice, practice and practice again, employing the verbs and making up sentences and speaking with them, so as to reinforce your memory of the verbs and so to make your command of them become second nature.

**Risking:** It is important to take the chance with Spanish conversation and use the verbs with (hopefully) the correct conjugations whenever an opportunity presents itself. Take the risk and speak with any Spanish speaker you may meet. You are bound to get your verbs wrong from time to time, but you should not allow anxiety about this to be a cause of failure to seize the chance to speak. As you use the verbs you will quickly become proficient.

**Reference:** As a further aid to impressing a new verb on the memory try looking it up it up in a dictionary (preferably a monolingual Spanish Dictionary) and checking the meaning. The translation of each verb provided in this book is necessarily brief and you may find from a dictionary that some other interpretations are possible.

**Recitation**: Recitation of the verb conjugations is similar to repetition in that it involves going over the verb several times, but with this difference: with recitation there is an attempt to recollect the verb conjugations and to repeat them just from memory. Recitation is important because it challenges the memory and in doing so makes a deeper impression upon it. You may not be successful all at once when trying to recite the verb conjugations, but by making the effort to remember (checking the original text version of the verb as need be to see if the effort was accurate and then trying again, as often as necessary) you will start to create a satisfactory strong memory of the verb.

After an initial period of reading and reflection on the verb and the conjugations you should be ready to start to try and memorize them.

Read over each tense of the selected verb in turn again and then try immediately to recall the conjugation of the tense from memory, repeating as necessary and checking and correcting yourself when in error. (Recitation). Work through each of the tenses for the selected verb in the same way.

Repeat a small selection of verbs every day over a period of several days and presently you will begin to remember the selection satisfactorily. Once you have few verbs at your fingertips, provided you are persistent, other verbs will begin to be easier to command.

# Chapter 23.
## The Lock-Step Method
### for Mastering and Recalling Spanish Verbs & Tenses

Follow the easy steps explained below you will soon become fluent with any and every Spanish verb.

The steps are based on the object of gaining an understanding of all the different tenses together as soon as possible, instead of spending undue amounts of time trying to be perfect with the use of one tense, before moving on the next, and so on. The traditional way to learn verbs in a foreign language is to take one tense, for example the present, and then to learn how to use the present tense with each of the various verb types, before proceeding to the next tense. Consequently beginners learning Spanish tend to overlearn the present tense and the future because these often appear early in text books and also are perceived to be easier.

The lock step method provides a different approach. It requires you to start learning **all** the tenses for a single verb type at once (and not to learn thoroughly of one tense at a time for all verbs types). This alternative approach is more active and avoids the risk of acquiring a mind-set for the obvious first tenses generally taught, and so becoming more proficient with these tenses than with others and relying unduly on them. The only variation to this learning method is with regard to the compound tenses that will be left to Step 4. This is because the compound tenses require the verb haber to be learned and that is the subject of Step 4.

Following the steps also makes learning easier because as well as starting to see all tenses equally, you will begin to notice patterns in the way a verb may develop. Additionally the step method reinforces what has been learned at each stage and emphasises the need to keep on learning and practising by conjugating further verbs.

**Daily Preliminary**.
Each day make a rapid skim reading of the chapters in this book covering the explanations as to how **all** the different verb tense forms and conjugations work and are used. The object with this reading is not to try and learn the material fully, but to develop an overview and to gain an understanding of where your study is going to take you. In this

way when you start to learn the different tenses you will be able to see them in context, and that will be a powerful aid to learning.

Next read in depth the explanation of at least one single different verb type and tenses. Start a new subject each day even though you may feel that the previous days study has not been fully grasped. Keep the cycle of a new subject per day going, until all have been covered and then return to the beginning and start again; in this way you will soon have an opportunity of revisiting any matters you may have found tricky.

**Step 1.**
Learn all the conjugations for the regular AR verbs using Hablar as your reference verb; but leaving out the compound verbs for the time being. Remember always to aim for accuracy and not speed.

Also take a different selection of other AR verbs each day and conjugate them in all their tenses.

**Step 2.**
Repeat Step 1 for regular ER verbs using Beber as your reference verb.

**Step 3.**
Repeat Step 1 for regular IR verbs using Discutir as your reference verb.

**Step 4.**
Learn the verb Haber and the use of the compound tenses. As you will see, you should immediately be able to conjugate the compound forms for Hablar, Beber, Discutir and for every other Spanish verb. Your daily selection of Spanish verbs can now cover all regular AR, ER and IR verbs as well as the compound tenses for all these verbs.

**Step 5.**
Learn about the verbs that have changes or irregularities for orthographic or euphonic reasons. In fact these types of verbs largely conform to obvious rules and the reasons for the changes will be obvious. With a good knowledge of the regular verb forms you should not find these verbs difficult to master. These types of verbs can now be added to your daily selection of verbs to conjugate.

**Step 6.**

Learn the verbs that are irregular due to Stem/Stress changes. Whilst these are not quite so easy as the verbs that change for orthographic or euphonic reasons, nonetheless there is often an underlying pattern to the irregularities. These types of verbs can also now be added to your daily selection of verbs to conjugate.

**Step 7.**
Learn the reflexive verb forms and add these to your daily selection.

**Step 8.**
Learn verbs that are completely irregular without any obvious pattern or rule. Your understanding of the regular verb forms will again be an aid, because even the truly irregular verbs may have something in common with the regular forms. With these irregular verbs learned you will be able to cope with any Spanish verb whether spoken or written.

**Step 9.**
When you have a good grasp of all verb forms, take a selection of verbs at random each day to study and conjugate. Always aim for accuracy and not for speed. Practice, more practice, patience and experience will bring perfection, and will also bring increased speed without any effort or need to worry about being quick. Make sure you are accurate and the speed will take care of itself.

Remember that the verbs should be used, not just learned. Do not let them become merely an intellectual exercise: press them into active service in conversations and writing as often as possible.

# Chapter 24
## Memory-tips, patterns and pointers
## for remembering Spanish verb conjugations.

1. The accent. The accent is a guide both to pronunciation and to the relevant tense. The correct accents should be considered in every conjugation. It is important always to get these right, so as to learn correctly, to understand correctly and to be understood when speaking.

2. O. The ending for the first person singular present tense verb types (AR, ER, IR) is O. The letter O is only otherwise used as the final letter of a verb ending in the preterite (past historic) tense where it always takes the accent (ó) except with some irregular verbs.

3. S, The second person singular of all tenses (other than the preterite/past historic and the imperative) and with all verb types (AR, ER, IR) has S as the final letter; (with other letters in the endings relevant to the particular tense/mood).

4. MOS. The first person plural (we/nosotros) in all verbs types (AR, ER, IR) and in all tenses/moods, has MOS as the final letters. (with other letters in the endings relevant to the particular tense/mood).

5. IS. The second person plural (you/vosotros) has IS as the final letters in all verb types (AR, ER, IR) and all tenses/moods other than the imperative positive-'do' (with other letters in the endings relevant to the particular tense/mood).

6. N. The third person plural (they/ellos) in in all tenses and with all verb types (AR, ER, IR) has N as the final letter. (with other letters in the endings relevant to the particular tense/mood).

7. ER and IR verbs. Verbs ending in ER and IR have identical endings in all tenses/moods and persons other than the first and second persons plural in the present tense and in the second person plural in the imperative.

8. The Imperfect. The imperfect tense is completely regular for all verbs except for Ir (to go), Ver (to see) and Ser (to be).

9. The Preterite (past historic). Note the similarity between the singular and the plural endings, the O ending that only occurs with this tense (with an accent) and with the present tense (the third person singular in the preterite tense and the first person singular in the present tense); also the MOS, the IS and the N endings, etc.

10. The Preterite (past historic). The first person plural (nosotros) is the same for the preterite as for the present tense with regular AR verbs and also with regular IR verbs. (This is not the case with regular ER verbs because they are the same as the IR verbs in the preterite).

11. The Preterite (past historic). Unless the pronouns are spoken as well, the only way to tell the difference between (Yo) hablo (present tense) and (Él) habló (preterite) is by noting the accent: and of course the pronouns are not always spoken if the person speaking is obvious from the conjugation (and correct pronunciation) of the verb.

12. The Future tense. The endings for the future tense are always regular, and only with the infinitive stem, to which they are added, are there ever any irregularities. These future tense irregularities are limited to the 12 irregular verbs following: DECIR, PONER, SALIR, VALER, QUERER, TENER, HACER, HABER, PODER, SABER, CABER, VENIR. For details of the future tense stem irregularities with these verbs see the chapter on the future tense.

Even with these 12 a pattern is evident. Note that the sound of the 12 irregular verbs in the future tense is made more comfortable by the irregularities. Try speaking them as they would otherwise be and the phonetic reason for the irregularities will be obvious. So the 12 irregular verbs should be easy to learn.

13. The Future tense and Haber. The present tense of haber is as follows: he, has, ha, hemos, habéis, han. The h is silent is Spanish, and when the h and the hab are deleted, you have the endings for the future tense.

14 The Conditional tense. The endings are the same for all verb types (AR, ER, IR).

15. The Conditional tense. The irregular verb stems are the same 12 as for the future tense (see above).

16. The Conditional tense and ER and IR verbs. The endings, although in a different place (ie attached to the infinitive) are the same as with the imperfect tense for er and ir verbs.

17. The Progressive tenses. Learn the Estar conjugations first.

18. The Progressive tenses. When learning the conjugations of any verb learn the participles at the same time. You will need the Present-Participle to form the progressive tenses and the Past-Participle to form the compound Haber tenses.

19. The Progressive tenses. The progressive tenses are easy to learn and use and have the advantage of flexibilty in that they can be used with the Present-Participle of any verb; and this is particularly helpful if perhaps the present or imperfect form of the relevant verb cannot be recalled.

20. The Present Subjunctive. Remember the clue generally given by the first person present indicative, Nearly always the irregular or stem changing verbs in the present subjunctive have the same stem as the verb in the first person present indicative.

21. The Present Subjunctive. AR verbs change their A for an E; and that ER and IR verbs change their E or I, for an A.

22. The Subjunctive. Whenever a sentence as to anything that is not a simple statement as to fact, is required, then consider whether the subjunctive should be used.

23. The Subjunctive. When reading anything in Spanish, if the subjunctive is encountered then always pause and work out why it was appropriate, and why the particular subjunctive tense was used. Keep a note book and make a list of the sentences found in this way, for future revision purposes.

24 The Imperfect Subjunctive. The imperfect subjunctive is formed by taking the third person plural (Ellos) of the preterite tense of the verb, removing the ending (which will be ARON for AR verbs and IERON for ER and IR verbs) and then applying the relevant endings. As to these see the chapter dealing with the Imperfect subjunctive.

25. The Future Subjunctive. This is not used at all now, so although you may come across it when reading older books, do not bother to learn it.

26. The Imperative. The accent for the imperative stays in the same place when pronouns are added on to the verb, as it would be if they had not been added.

27. The Imperative. Apart from the Tú and Vosotros forms, the imperative borrows from the present subjunctive. So it will be helpful to master the present subjunctive before learning the imperative.

28. The Imperative. The dropping of the S from MOS in reflexive verb forms for Nosotros and the dropping of the D in the reflexive verb forms for Vosotros are clearly the result of the more comfortable sound achieved. For example: 'Peinémosnos' and 'Peinados' would sound somewhat clumsy.

# Part Three: The Most Useful and Essential Spanish Verbs

## Chapter 25
### The 151 Essential Spanish Verbs
### Learn these and you will be able to understand, and to make yourself understood in Spanish in all everyday situations.

The prospect of studying numerous verbs may be a little daunting for those who are just beginning to study Spanish. However set out below is a list of the 151 best verbs to study first. The list is designed to provide enough verbs so that you will be able to make oneself understood and to get by in all everyday situations (travel, easy conversations, etc.) in the language.

By using the memorising methods explained in the preceding chapters of this book you should not find it difficult to master the 151 and you will then have a excellent foundation from which to go on to any other verb in Spanish; because of course, with your grasp of the 151, you will find that you naturally go on acquiring, and knowing how to conjugate, almost by assimilation, more verbs, which you will gather from reading in Spanish and from talking with Spanish speakers.

With each verb there is a letter, A, B or C. The A verbs are more or less the most important to learn initially, then the B verbs and finally the Cs, but really all should be learned.

The 151 list also provides a very good range of the different verb types that will be encountered generally. When you can understand and can conjugate the 151 verbs you should be able to cope with very nearly every type of verb, however it may be conjugated, regular ofrirregular although not for example those that would be encountered not very frequently.

The set of fully conjugated verbs which are provided in the companion volume to this book **Spanish Verb Perfect**, provides models for all the 151 (see the conjugation guide below) as well as models for all possible variations of conjugations for all Spanish verbs.

## Key to abbreviations:
R= Regular
O= Changes mostly Orthographic/Euphonic
S= Stem changes
RF= Reflexive
I= Irregular
M= Mixed changes/irregularities
Ú/Í= Stem U or stem I verb with stress changes
DC= Conjugation derived from some other verb
Past-P= Past-Participle
Pres P= Present-Participle
O/W = Otherwise
D= Defective, incomplete or impersonal verb. Only available in some conjugations.

A model for each of the verbs indicated in the Conjugation Guide column can be found, fully conjugated, in **Spanish Verb Perfect,** the companion volume to this book. Note the verb participles (especially the handful of irregular past participles) and then conjugate each verb exactly as the verb shown in the Conjugation Guide is conjugated.

| Verb | Participles | Conjugation Guide |
|---|---|---|
| **Abandonar: to leave to abandon - C** | abandonando abandonado | R-Hablar |
| **Abrazar: to embrace, to hug - C** | abrazando abrazado | O-Rezar |
| **Abrir: to open - B** | abriendo abierto | Note Ireg Past P O/W R-Discutir |
| **Acabar: to finish, to end - B** | acabando acabado | R-Hablar |

| | | |
|---|---|---|
| **Aceptar: to accept, to take - B** | aceptando aceptado | R-Hablar |
| **Admirar: to admire - C** | admirando admirado | R-Hablar |
| **Aguardar: to wait for - C** | aguardando aguardado | R-Hablar |
| **Andar: to walk - A** | andando andado | I-Andar |
| **Aprender: to learn - A** | aprendiendo aprendido | R-Beber |
| **Asistir: to assist, to attend - B** | asistiendo asistido | R-Discutir |
| **Bailar: to dance - C** | bailando bailado | R-Hablar |
| **Bajar: to go down, to descend - C** | bajando bajado | R-Hablar |
| **Beber: to drink - A** | bebiendo bebido | R-Beber |
| **Besar: to kiss - C** | besando besado | R-Hablar |
| **Burlar: to deceive, to trick - C** | burlando burlado | R-Hablar |
| **Burlarse: to mock, to make fun of - B** | Burlandose burlado | R-RF-Levantarse |
| **Buscar: to look for - A** | buscando buscado | O-Tocar |
| **Caber: to fit, to accommodate A** | cabiendo cabido | I-Caber |
| **Caer: to fall - A** | cayendo caído | O-Caer |
| **Caerse: to fall - A** | cayéndose caído | I-RF-Caerse |
| **Cambiar: to change - B** | cambiando cambiado | R-Hablar |
| **Cantar: to sing - B** | cantando cantado | R-Hablar |
| **Callarse:to shut up/to be silent B** | callándose callado | R-RF-Levantarse |
| **Carecer: to lack - C** | careciendo carecido | O-Conocer |
| **Casarse: to marry - C** | casándose casado | R-RF-Levantarse |

| | | |
|---|---|---|
| **Cerrar: to close - A** | cerrando cerrado | S-Alentar- |
| **Cobrar: to charge, to collect - C** | cobrando cobrado | R-Hablar |
| **Cocinar: to cook - B** | cocinando cocinado | R-Hablar |
| **Coger: to take, to catch, to seize - A** | cogiendo cogido | O-Escoger |
| **Comenzar: to commence, to begin - B** | comenzando comenzado | M Comenzar |
| **Comer: to eat - A** | comiendo comido | R-Beber |
| **Compartir: to share, to divide up - C** | compartiendo compartido | R-Discutir |
| **Comprar: to buy - A** | comprando comprado | R-Hablar |
| **Conducir: to lead, to conduct - B** | conduciendo conducido | M-Producir |
| **Conocer: to know, to meet - B** | conociendo conocido | O-Conocer |
| **Construir: to build, to construct - B** | construyendo construido | O-Instruir |
| **Contar: to tell, to relate - A** | contando contado | S-Aprobar |
| **Correr: to run - B** | corriendo corrido | R-Beber |
| **Cortar: to cut, to crop - B** | cortando cortado | R-Hablar |
| **Costar: to cost - A** | costando costado | D R-S-Costar |
| **Creer: to believe - A** | creyendo creído | O-Creer |
| **Cuidarse: to take care of oneself - B** | cuidándose cuidado | R-RF-Levantarse |
| **Dar: to give - A** | dando dado | I-Dar |
| **Deber: to owe, to have to - A** | debiendo debido | R-Beber |
| **Decidir: to decide, to determine - B** | decidiendo decidido | R-Discutir |

| | | |
|---|---|---|
| **Decir: to say, to tell - A** | diciendo dicho | I-Decir |
| **Defenderse: to defend oneself - C** | defendiéndose defendido | S-RF-Defenderse |
| **Desayunarse: to breakfast, to have breadfast -C** | desayunándose desayunado | R-RF-Levantarse |
| **Descansar: to rest - B** | descansado descansado | R-Hablar |
| **Desear: to desire, to wish - B** | deseando deseado | R-Hablar |
| **Despedirse -C** | despidiéndose despedido | S-RF-Despedirse |
| **Desvestirse -C** | desvistiéndose desvestido | S-RF-Desvestirse |
| **Detener: to stop, to detain - C** | deteniendo detenido | I-Tener |
| **Dormir: to sleep - A** | durmiendo dormido | S-Dormir |
| **Dudar: to doubt - B** | dudando dudado | R-Hablar |
| **Echar: to throw, to cast - B** | echando echado | R-Hablar |
| **Empezar: to employ, to use - A** | empezando empezado | M-Empezar |
| **Emplear: to employ, to use - B** | empleando empleado | R-Hablar |
| **Encantar: to delight, to charm - B** | encantando encantado | R-Hablar |
| **Encontrar: to find, to encounter - A** | encontrando encontrado | S-Aprobar |
| **Enseñar: to teach, to instruct - B** | enseñando enseñado | R-Hablar |
| **Entender: to understand - A** | entendiendo entendido | S- Entender |
| **Entrar: to enter - B** | entrando entrado | R-Hablar |

| | | |
|---|---|---|
| **Enviar: to send, to dispatch - B** | enviando enviado | Ú/Í-Ampliar |
| **Escribir: to write - A** | escribiendo escrito | Note Ireg Past P O/W R-Discutir |
| **Escuchar: to listen, to hear - B** | escuchando escuchado | R-Hablar |
| **Esperar: to hope, to wait, to expect - A** | esperando esperado | R-Hablar |
| **Estar: to be - A** | estando estando | I-Estar |
| **Estudiar: to study - B** | estudiando estudiado | R-Hablar |
| **Fiar: to entrust, to confide - C** | fiando fiado | Ú/Í-Ampliar |
| **Firmar: to sign - B** | firmando firmado | R-Hablar |
| **Ganar: to gain, to earn, to win - B** | ganando ganado | R-Hablar |
| **Gastar: to spend, to consume - B** | gastando gastado | R-Hablar |
| **Gozar: to enjoy - C** | gozando gozado | O-Rezar |
| **Gustar: to please (to like), to taste - A** | gustando gustado | D R-Hablar |
| **Haber:to have(auxillary verb)- A** | habiendo habido | I-Haber |
| **Hablar: to talk, to speak - A** | hablando hablado | R-Hablar |
| **Hacer: to make, to create - A** | haciendo hecho | I-Hacer |
| **Hambrear: to starve - C** | hambreando hambreado | R-Hablar |
| **Imaginarse: to imagine, to fancy - C** | imaginándose imaginado | R-RF-Levantarse |
| **Intentar: to try, to attempt - B** | intentando intentado | R-Hablar |
| **Ir: to go/to go away - A** | yendo ido | I-Ir |
| **Irse: to go/to go away - A** | yéndose ido | I-RF-Irse |

| Jugar: to play, to gamble - B | jugando jugado | S-Jugar |
|---|---|---|
| Labrar: to work, to carve - C | labrando labrado | R-Hablar |
| Llamarse: to be called -B | Llamándose llamado | R-RF-Levantarse |
| Lavarse: to wash/ o.s - C | lavándose lavado | R-RF-Levantarse |
| Leer: to read - A | leyendo leído | O-Creer |
| Llenar: to fill - C | llenando llenado | R-Hablar |
| Llegar: to arrive, to reach - A | llegando llegado | O-Pagar |
| Llevar: to carry, to lead, to wear - B | llevando llevado | R-Hablar |
| Llover: to rain - C | lloviendo llovido | D S Remover |
| Mentir: to lie - B | mintiendo mentido | S-Sentir |
| Mirar: to look at. - A | mirando mirado | R-Hablar |
| Mirarse: to look at. o.s- A | mirándose mirado | R-RF-Levantarse |
| Morir: to die - C | muriendo muerto | S- Morir |
| Mostrar: to show, to display - B | mostrando mostrado | S-Aprobar- |
| Nacer: to be born - C | naciendo nacido | O-Conocer |
| Necesitar: to need - B | necesitando necesitado | R-Hablar |
| Oir: to hear, to listen to - A | oyendo oído | I-Oir |
| Olvidar: to forget - C | olvidando olvidado | R-Hablar |
| Pagar: to pay - A | pagando pagado | O-Pagar |
| Parar: to stop - C | parando parado | R-Hablar |
| Partir: to set of, to go away, to depart - B | partir partido | R-Discutir |
| Pasar: to pass, to happen - A | pasando pasando | R-Hablar |
| Pasearse: to walk/: to go for a walk - C | paseándose paseado | R-RF-Levantarse |

| | | |
|---|---|---|
| **Pedir: to ask for, to request - B** | pidiendo pedido | Note Ireg Pres P O/W S-Servir- |
| **Pensar: to think - A** | pensando pensado | S-Alentar-Acertar |
| **Perder: to lose, to waste - B** | perdiendo perdido | S-Perder-Entender |
| **Permitir: to permit, to allow - C** | permitiendo permitido | R-Discutir |
| **Placer: to please - C** | placiendo placido | O-Conocer |
| **Poder: to be able - A** | pudiendo podido | I-Poder |
| **Poner: to put, to place - B** | poniendo puesto | I-Poner |
| **Practicar: to practise, to go in for - C** | practicando practicado | O-Tocar |
| **Preferir: to prefer - C** | prefiriendo preferido | S-Sentir-Advertir |
| **Preguntar: to ask, to enquire - A** | preguntando preguntado | R-Hablar |
| **Preocuparse: to care/ to worry about - C** | preocupándose preocupado | R-RF-Levantarse |
| **Prohibir: to prohibit, to ban - C** | prohibiendo prohibido | Ú/Í-Prohibir |
| **Quedar: to stay, to remain - C** | quedando quedado | R-Hablar |
| **Quedarse: to stay, to remain - C** | quedándose quedado | R-RF-Levantarse |
| **Quejarse: to complain - B** | quejándose quejado | R-RF-Levantarse |
| **Querer: to want, to wish, to like - A** | queriendo querido | I-Querer |
| **Recibir: to receive, to welcome - C** | recibiendo recibido | R-Discutir |
| **Regalar: to give away, to give a present -B** | regalando regalado | R-Hablar |
| **Regresar: to go back, to return - C** | regresando regresado | R-Hablar |
| **Reirse: to laugh at - B** | riéndose reído | S-RF-Reírse |

| | | |
|---|---|---|
| **Responder: to answer, to reply to - B** | respondiendo respondido | R-Beber |
| **Robar: to rob - C** | robando robado | R-Hablar |
| **Romper: to break - C** | rompiendo roto | Note Ireg Past P O/W R-Beber |
| **Saber: to know - A** | sabiendo sabido | I-Saber |
| **Sacar: to take out/to withdraw C** | sacando sacado | O-Tocar |
| **Salir: to go out, to leave - A** | saliendo salido | I-Salir |
| **Seguir: to follow, to continue -B** | siguiendo seguido | M-Seguir |
| **Sentirse: to feel, to sense/ to feel regret - B** | sintiéndose sentido | S-RF-Sentirse |
| **Sentarse: to sit o.s. down - C** | sentándose sentado | S-RF-Sentarse |
| **Ser: to be - A** | siendo sido | I-Ser |
| **Servir: to serve, to help - C** | sirviendo servido | S-Servir-Competir |
| **Sorprender: to surprise, to astonish - C** | sorprendiendo sorprendido | R-Beber |
| **Subir: to go up, to climb, to raise - B** | subiendo subido | R-Discutir |
| **Tardar: to delay, to take time - C** | tardando tardado | R-Hablar |
| **Tener: to have, to possess - A** | teniendo tenido | I-Tener |
| **Terminar: to end, to finish - B** | terminando terminado | R-Hablar |
| **Tirar: to throw, to throw away - C** | tirando tirado | R-Hablar |
| **Tocar: to touch, to play - B** | tocando tocado | O-Tocar |
| **Tomar: to take, to have - B** | tomando tomado | R-Hablar |
| **Trabajar: to work - A** | trabajando trabajado | R-Hablar |

| | | |
|---|---|---|
| **Traer: to bring, to carry - C** | trayendo traído | I-Traer |
| **Usar: to use - B** | usando usado | R-Hablar |
| **Valer: to be worth, to avail, to help - A** | valiendo valido | I-Valer |
| **Vencer: to conquer, to defeat - C** | venciendo vencido | O-Vencer |
| **Vender: to sell - B** | vendiendo vendido | R-Beber |
| **Venir: to come - A** | viniendo venido | I-Venir |
| **Ver: to see - A** | viendo visto | I-Ver |
| **Viajar: to journey, to travel - A** | viajando viajado | R-Hablar |
| **Vivir: to live - A** | viviendo vivido | R-Discutir |
| **Volver: to return, to turn - A** | volviendo vuelto | Note Ireg Past P O/W S-Remover |

## Conclusion

Good luck with your Spanish studies; and if you have found this book helpful please would you leave a positive review.

These are some of my other books:

*How to learn - Spanish - French - German - Arabic - any foreign language successfully.*
*and*
*How To Transform Your Memory & Brain Power: Power-Learn, Memorize & Remember Anything.*
*and*
*How I Learned To Speak Spanish Fluently In Three Months: Discover How You Can Conquer Spanish Easily The Same Way.*
*and*
*Dual Language First Spanish Reader. Spanish-English Short Stories for Beginners*
*and*
*Dual Language Spanish Reader. Parallel Spanish-English Short Stories. Level Beginner to Intermediate*
*and*
*Spanish Verb Perfect: Fully Conjugated Models for Every Type Of Spanish Verb*

CPSIA information can be obtained
at www.ICGtesting.com
Printed in the USA
LVHW031506310120
645463LV00002B/368